1. 31. 79

CHINESE COOKING FOR AMERICAN KITCHENS

Wenchin Yu Hsiung

中國烹飪

Aurora Publishers, Inc.
Nashville, Tennessee

Library of Congress Cataloging in Publication Data

Hsiung, Wenchin Yu.
  Chinese cooking for American kitchens.

  Includes index.
  1. Cookery, Chinese, I. Title.
TX724.5.C5H73   641.5'951   77-25543
ISBN 0-87695-218-X

ISBN 87695 218-X (Paper)
ISBN 87695 219-8 (Comb)
ISBN 87695 220-1 (Board)

For my husband, Chuan-Chih

and my daughter, Nancy

Without their enthusiasm,

encouragement and help this book

would never have been written

Contents

Preface

Food is essential to everyone. More than four thousand years ago, the Emperor Fu Hsi introduced agricultural techniques and domestication of animals to the Chinese people. Since then, the Chinese people have developed a philosophy about food: Cooking delicious as well as nutritious foods contributes to the health and happiness of every family in every position and profession of life. Hundreds of years have been spent experimenting with the various aspects of what actually makes food good.

There are advantages other than its distinct tastes to cooking Chinese food. Centuries of using coal, wood and charcoal as heat sources had contributed to the diminishing fuel supply as the population increased. The Chinese people developed methods of cooking that took little time (such as stir-frying) and low heat (such as stewing and steaming). In our present state of energy shortage, cooking Chinese food would save a significant amount of fuel as well as providing delicious and nutritious food. Furthermore Chinese food is high in nutrients and low in calories, an advantage to health- and weight-conscious people.

The primary reason for cooking Chinese food is, of course, its widely varied and highly creative cuisine. The essence of Chinese cooking lies in the traditional insistance that food must have color, aroma, and above all, flavor. In order to achieve these purposes we have to pay attention to the proper cooking-timing (huo-hou), the freshness and tenderness of ingredients, the proper cutting methods, the cooking utensils and the kind of stoves.

Ideally Chinese food is cooked using a Chinese wok and a gas stove. I have an electric stove and a number of pots and pans made of stainless steel and Teflon. Originally, I made a special trip to Chinatown to buy a wok, complete with ring and cover. Unfortunately the wok did not fit on the burners of my stove. This prompted my decision to adjust Chinese cooking to fit any type of stove and any kind of cooking utensil. The end result is that my recipes can be used in any average American kitchen.

Encouraged by my husband and my daughter who have given me immeasurable help and encouragement, I set out to write a cookbook to share my experiments with people who want to cook and eat Chinese food, but hesitate to try.

In addition to thanking my husband and daughter for their support, I also want to express my appreciation to my cousin Mrs. I-chi Kung Hsiung for the illustration and all my friends who gave me good advice and help.

WENCHIN YU HSIUNG

1

INTRODUCTION

China is a big country. Due to the geographical divisions and climatic differences, Chinese cooking varies in flavor and aroma in the different regions. Hence Chinese food can be grouped into five regions.

1. Northern Region: The Peking-Shantung cooking is distinguished by light, elegant, mildly-seasoned rather than rich food and the liberal use of garlic, scallions, leeks and chives. There are famous delicacies such as Peking duck and Moo-Shi meat.

2. Eastern Region: Shanghai, Yangchow, and Fukien. There are three styles of cooking in this region. Shanghai cooking is cosmopolitan, a combination of the cooking of all the regions. In Yangchow—called the Paris of China—many foods are preserved in salt. A famous delicacy is the Yangchow steamed dumpling. In contrast, Fukien cooking is famous for seafood and for clear, light soups.

3. Western Region: Szechuan and Yuennan. The sharpness of its flavors and the sting of its spices are achieved through the use of ginger, garlic, Szechuan peppercorns and hot peppers. Famous delicacies in Szechuan include Pon Pon chicken and Szechuan roast duck while Hsian Vi (宣威) ham is famous in Yuennan.

4. Southern Region: Kwangtung. The Cantonese cooking is very popular in the West. It is noted for roast meats and poultry and Cantonese lobster. The famous delicacies, bird's nest soup and shark's fin soup, originated in this region.

5. Central Region: Hunan. Rich seasonings such as spiced sauces and sweet and sour flavorings are characteristics of the Hunan region. A famous dish of this area is the yellow river carp.

The recipes in my book are not classified by regional styles but rather are divided by categories such as beef, poultry, seafood and so on. This will facilitate selection of menus containing the proper balance of various courses.

Chinese cooking calls for maximum preparation and minimum cooking. Chinese spend more time preparing and less time cooking (especially when stir-frying). Meat is never tough but always exceedingly tender, poultry is never dry but always savory and juicy, vegetables are never overdone but crisp and crunchy, and rich dishes are not too rich and never greasy.

Many factors contribute to the culinary art of Chinese cooking—the food ingredients, cutting and chopping skills, kitchen utensils, cooking range, and cooking methods. Each of these will be described in detail in the following sections.

I. THE INGREDIENTS

Ingredients are usually combined, seldom cooked alone. The higher the level of cooking, the more superb and perfect this blending becomes. Yet with a given dish the individuality of each ingredient is never lost; its taste and texture are always retained. Its individual flavor must always be brought out. In other words in Chinese cooking the cook not the diner seasons the food, and the cook not the diner cuts the food.

1. The main ingredients

Meat: Pork is the staple and supreme Chinese meat. The best cuts for cooking are pork tenderloin, Boston butt and country style spareribs. In the United States we also use beef. The good cuts to use are flank steak, round steak and beef fillet.

Poultry: Chicken and duck are the most common poultry in Chinese dishes.

Seafood: Both fresh and salt water seafood such as shrimp, fish, crab and lobster are used.

Vegetables: The Chinese cook with nearly all vegetables known to Americans as well as a number of others which are uniquely Chinese, such as bean sprouts, bamboo shoots and water chestnuts.

Grain: Both wheat and rice are found in Chinese cuisine and especially utilized in pastries.

Fruit: Snacks and desserts are often comprised of common fruits. Besides the fruits grown here, we select Chinese fruits such as loquats and lichee.

Nuts: Walnuts, cashews, almonds and peanuts are used to add special flavors to many dishes.

2. Essential seasonings and condiments

Soy sauce: The most important seasoning in Chinese cooking is soy sauce. Chinese and Japanese soy sauces are the most common. In most of my recipes La Choy and Japanese soy sauce are used because they are not as salty as the imported Chinese soy sauce. There are two kinds of imported Chinese soy sauces: 生抽 Sang Chou is light and good for stir-frying, while 老抽 Lou Chou is dark and good for stewing, i.e., red-cooking. If you use them please adjust the quantity of soy sauce in the recipe (to your taste) because they are saltier than La Choy and Japanese soy sauce.

Oil: In China, lard and peanut oil are most commonly used, but I think that lard is too fatty and the slightly better taste using peanut oil does not compensate for its high cost. Most of my recipes utilize vegetable oil and corn oil.

Salt: The Chinese use rough salt and fine salt in Chinese cooking. I find that

2

the regular salt sold in the supermarket works very well.

Vinegar: I use white vinegar in my recipes.

Sugar: The common sugars are brown, white and crystal sugars (rock candy).

Wine: Although rice wine is the best wine for Chinese cooking, sherry is an excellent substitute.

Starch: There are different kinds of starches made from water chestnuts, potato, flour or corn in Chinese cooking. I use the cornstarch sold in the supermarket.

Stocks: Stocks are obtained from chicken or pork or their bones. Most of my recipes utilize chicken stock or store-bought chicken broth.

Gourmet powder: In Chinese cooking monosodium glutamate is very commonly used. Most of my recipes contain monosodium glutamate (or Aćcent), but it is optional.

Pepper: There are two kinds of peppers, black pepper and white pepper. Chinese mostly cook with white pepper. Either black or white pepper can be used in my recipes.

Hot pepper: Aromatic red hot pepper and Szechuan hot pepper paste are used in seasoning stir-fried dishes.

Garlic: Fresh garlic is always found in Chinese cooking. I prefer fresh garlic for my recipes. In case you do not have any on hand, you can temporarily use garlic powder (not as desirable in its place). One chopped fresh garlic is about equal to the amount of ¼ teaspoon of ground garlic powder.

Ginger: Chinese cooking always uses ginger root. I prefer fresh ginger root for my recipes. If you cannot get fresh ginger, you can temporarily substitute ¼ teaspoon ginger powder for 1 tablespoon chopped fresh ginger (not as desirable).

Sesame oil: A strong, aromatic and fragrant oil, used as a flavoring. A few drops will improve any dish.

Mustard: A very strong and hot powder or paste is used sparingly.

Scallions (or onions): Scallions are cooked directly in hot oil to extract their flavor or put in soup and cold-mixing dishes.

Star anise: An eight-pointed star is usually added to flavor red-cooked meat and poultry dishes.

Dried black fermented beans: These have a strong, pungent salty smell. After having been presoaked in hot water for about 15 minutes, the dried beans are then ready to be added as a seasoning.

Hoisin sauce: A thick dark brown sauce is used in cooking dishes such as roast pork, barbecue spareribs and a dip sauce for Peking duck.

Chili sauce and ketchup: They were not found in Chinese cooking before this century. They are now used frequently in Chinese recipes.

3. For garnishes

The ingredients which are used for garnishes are nuts, mushrooms, scallions, dried shrimps, bamboo shoots, Chinese parsley, sesame seeds, deep-fried rice, flour noodles and Smithfield ham, lettuce or fried eggs cut in narrow strips.

II. CUTTING AND CHOPPING SKILLS

Skill in cutting and chopping is important for Chinese cooking because small pieces are easily stirred and cooked faster. Cooking small pieces also saves fuel and improves the flavor. When you start to prepare Chinese food, first clean the ingredients if needed. Then cut them into different shapes by slicing, shredding, dicing or mincing, depending on the recipe. The different cutting skills are described in detail in the following sections.

1. Slicing

Soft and tender ingredients such as mushrooms must be sliced straight or vertically. Diagonal slicing or slicing at an angle are applied to tough vegetables or coarse grained meat such as London broil (beef). When cylindrical vegetables such as carrots or asparagus are cut, the rolling knife cutting method is used. That is, first cut it at an angle of 30° from the axis. Roll the rest of the carrot about 120° and cut it at 30° from the axis again so that the new cut will partly cut across the original cut surface and partly across a new surface. Repeating the right slant, the right amount of rolling and right length of advance produce beautiful combinations of parts of curved cylindrical and plane elliptical surfaces.

2. Dicing

First cut the ingredients into strips: then cross cut into dices. For deep frying or stewing (red-cooking) the ingredients are cut into big dices (called cubes) about half inch to two inches. For stir-frying the ingredients are cut into small dices about one-eighth inch to half inch. For steaming the ingredients are diced into one-sixteenth to one-eighth inch cubes.

3. Shredding

For steaming and stir-frying, the ingredients are sliced and then each slice is cut into shreds. If the ingredients are cut 2 to 3 inches in length, ½ inch wide and ⅛ inch thick, they are called Julienne strips (also matchsticks). If the strips are not so precise, they are called slivers. Strips that are 2 to 3 inches in length but thinner and narrower are called threadlike strips.

4. Mincing

For frying or steaming meat balls, the ingredients must be cut in one direction and then in another, cross hatching continuously until they look almost like machine ground.

I always buy lean Boston (or pork) butt and ask the butcher at the meat counter to take off the fat and the bone and to grind the meat through the machine once (only once) on the coarse setting.

5. Crushing

For stir-frying, the seasoning ingredients such as ginger and garlic are often crushed. Garlic can be crushed with back of the knife, the butt of the knife handle, the bottom of a jar or the cleaver blade parallel to the cutting board. Ginger should first be cut into ½ inch thick slices, and then each slice is hit firmly with the side of the knife.

6. Scoring

Scoring is used for a whole fish or a large cut of meat or ham. A few light incisions are made (either parallel or cross hatch) in the surface to permit hot oil and seasoning to penetrate. This method speeds up cooking and improves the flavor.

III. COOKING UTENSILS AND STOVE

The traditional basic Chinese utensils are the wok, cleaver and chopsticks. The other Chinese utensils include the bamboo steamer, long handle scoop ladle, curved spatula, perforated scoop and perforated heavy metal round sieve. Other utensils considered of use are the Chinese "Hot pot" or tea pot, etc. Using the wok to cook Chinese food is the ideal way, but Western pots and pans (including Teflon pots and pans) are perfectly fine for Chinese cooking. Western pans and pots are better than the wok on electric stoves because of their flat bottoms which distribute the heat evenly to the food. Any kind of pot (including pressure cooker without the pressure cap on) can be used for stewing dishes such as red-cooked or white-cooked meats. Since some stewing dishes will take several hours to simmer, faster cooking can be obtained with a pressure cooker without the pressure cap on. This will be faster than regular stewing but not as fast as that with the cap on. However, if the food is cooked too fast (with the pressure cap on), the ingredients will not get the flavor from the seasonings and the sauce. Therefore even if the food was done quickly, it will not be very tasty.

When steaming is required, a regular steamer can be purchased from a Chinese grocery, or a covered pot containing a rack which stands above 2 or 3 inches of water can be used. The ingredients are placed in a heatproof dish or plate and put on the rack. Alternatively, a big heatproof bowl can be put at the bottom of a big pot with a cover. The pot should be a little bigger than the bowl to allow the water vapor through.

Although a gas stove is best for cooking Chinese food, if certain adjustments are made, the electric stove is just as good. When I need high heat for Chinese cooking, I always turn on medium high heat, instead of high heat, on my electric stove. There are three reasons for my doing this. First of all it will take about 1 to 2 minutes to get the burner to high heat and also take about 6 to 7 minutes to cool down. Using medium high heat will take less time and less energy. Second of all, when you cook stir-frying dishes, cooking-timing is so important. When the dish is done, the pan should be immediately lifted off the stove. With medium high heat, the heat is not so intense as in high heat and it is easier to start cooking another dish on the stove. Do not turn the switch on and off—save time and energy. Third of all the cook can use Teflon pans and pots (which are not good over high heat) to cook Chinese food; these are ideal for stir-frying dishes with less oil because the food has less tendency to stick to the pot or pan.

Western utensils can be adapted to Chinese cooking. A pair of chopsticks, a regular spatula, or a large spoon will do the stir-fry as well as a special Chinese curved spatula or long handled scoop. Colanders and strainers can replace the long handled perforated scoop and the heavy round metal sieve. A hand can opener does a better job of opening Chinese food cans than electric can openers because of the irregular size of the tops of foreign made cans. A big electric deep fryer or an electric deep-frying pan can be used to replace the Chinese "Hot pot."

It is convenient to have a pair of heavy and light cleavers as well as a mallet for cutting bones and tender ingredients. The ordinary Western sharp knives can do the general cutting job. I always have a knife sharpener on hand. Certainly a good and heavy wood chopping board is necessary. In short, all the Western kitchen utensils are good for Chinese cooking.

IV. THE COOKING METHODS

The cooking-timing (Huo-hou 火候) is the most important factor in Chinese cooking. An excellent Chinese cook is a master in knowing how to adjust cooking-timing when she (he) cooks. There are more than thirty ways to cook Chinese food. Let me just mention several of the more common techniques.

1. Stir-frying

The key to stir-frying is the cooking-timing (the intensity of the cooking heat). Stir-frying is similar to sautéing, but it is much more rapid and interesting. Stir-frying can be accomplished by quickly stirring a spoon or a spatula down between the food and the pan with a scraping and tossing motion. Stir-frying may seem difficult at first but practice and experience make it increasingly easy and enjoyable.

When the cooking is done, *lift* the pan off of the stove if using an electric stove or turn off the burner if using a gas stove. Then transfer the food to a serving plate. Serve immediately. Stir-fried dishes should never be kept on the stove until the diners are seated at the table. There is a Chinese proverb: "Better that a man should wait for his meal than the meal should wait for the man" ("『寧人等粥勿粥等人』").

Besides the importance of cooking-timing, successful stir-frying needs very careful preparation. Read the recipe well in advance, and know which ingredients are needed. Allow time to soak the dry ingredients and to parboil vegetables. Plan to wash and cut the meat, seasonings and vegetables with enough time to marinade or dredge the ingredients. Mix the seasonings in separate bowls and blend the cornstarch with water if needed, before the cooking starts. Arrange everything on a table or a counter near the stove. When the actual cooking process starts, it will only last a few minutes.

2. Deep frying

There are two kinds of deep frying.

i. Single frying. The heat for deep frying should be reduced slightly once the ingredients are in the pot (otherwise the outside will be charred before the inside is cooked). When using an electric deep fryer, set the temperature to about 350°F. After some of the ingredients are put into the fryer turn to 325°F for a short while. Then turn back to 350°F until the ingredients are done. For any pot on an electric stove, turn to medium high heat. When the oil is hot, drop a piece of bread into the oil. When the bread bubbles, the oil is the right temperature for deep frying. After adding the ingredients, turn the heat to medium until the ingredients are half done. Then turn to medium high and continue cooking until done. Repeat the same process for the rest of the ingredients. (With a gas stove or any pot which is not Teflon, high then medium heat can be used.)

ii. Double frying. When the oil is hot and the right temperature, immerse the ingredients briefly in the hot oil until pale golden. Then remove and cool the ingredients while the oil itself is reheated. Return the ingredients to oil, and cook until done. (This method produces crispier ingredients and also keeps the outside from cooking too quickly, before the inside is done.)

Preparing the ingredients for deep frying in Chinese cooking differs from Western methods. The ingredients are often marinated first in soy sauce, sherry and seasonings from 30 minutes to several hours before dipping into the batter consisting of cornstarch flour and other ingredients.

The ingredients for deep frying can be whole or cut into medium-sized pieces. When deep frying, do not put all the medium-sized pieces in at once, only a few at a time. Because of this, a large quantity of oil is not needed to deep-fry the small pieces of ingredients; a depth of 3 or 4 inches oil in your pot is enough for your cooking.

The oil which you used to cook the ingredients can be saved and reused several times. If the oil is reused, add some new oil into it, if needed. However, if the oil is used for frying fish, only reuse it for frying fish because of the strong odor that is retained in the oil. Similarly, if the oil is used for frying shrimp, only reuse that oil for frying shrimp.

3. Steaming

The ingredients for steaming are cooked by water vapor, or steam. After the cooking is done, the ingredients will retain their flavor and their own juices.

Chinese steaming can be done in several ways (see also the second paragraph of Section III in chapter 1):

  i. Use a regular steamer which you can get from a Chinese grocery.
 ii. Use a rack which stands above 2 or 3 inches of water in a pot with cover. The ingredients are placed in a heatproof dish or plate which is placed on the rack.
iii. Use a big heatproof bowl which is put at the bottom of a covered pot. The ingredients are placed in the big bowl with cover. Pour boiling water about one half of the height of the bowl. This is special for the big ingredients such as a whole chicken or duck. Put the pot over medium high heat (using a gas stove or a pot which is not Teflon, high heat can be used). When the water boils, reduce to medium or low heat, just enough to maintain the boiling. The pot should be big enough to permit the steam to circulate.

During the steaming time, the cook should check the water in the steamer or the pot. If it has diminished too much, replenish it with boiling water.

4. Stewing

There are two kinds of stewing: white-stewing and red-cooking.

  i. White-stewing, also called clear simmering, does not use any soy sauce, and is used with whole poultry, large cut meats and bite-sized cuts of poultry or meat. First, put the ingredients in boiling water; this will seal in juices and make the meat tastier. Then drain, throwing away the water, and put the ingredients in the pot again with cold water with a few pieces of ginger. When the water boils, reduce the heat at once to a simmer. As fat and impurities rise to the surface, skim them off until they no longer accumulate. Cover the pot and simmer 1 to 2 hours depending on the size of the ingredients.
 ii. Red-cooking. The meat becomes red-brown in color with brown gravy produced by soy sauce. This type of stewing is also used with whole poultry, large cut meats and bite-sized cuts of poultry or meat. Then put it in the pot with soy sauce, ginger, star anise and water over medium high heat. When the sauce boils, add sherry and reduce to low heat and simmer. Before the meat is done, add sugar. Sometimes the meat is fried first with seasonings added and then red-cooked. Red-cooked meat can be refrigerated and reheated as well as served chilled. When refrigerated, the red-cooked sauce becomes jellied like aspic.

5. Roasting

The meat or poultry for Chinese roasting is always marinated by soy sauce or a highly seasoned marinade for several hours or overnight and basted frequently during the roasting time. The roasting method involves either using a roasting pan or putting the meat on a rack or hanging the meat on a wire from the top of the oven with a pan of water underneath to catch the dripping and prevent charring.

6. Salting and drying

Since fuel and food have been scarce for centuries, nutritious foods have been preserved for the winter or lean times. Furthermore, there was no refrigerator or canning in most parts of China in the past. So drying, fermenting, pickling, salting and sugaring were the skillful ways to preserve food. These methods are still economical and sometimes yield foods that are tastier than freshly prepared.

Drying is more difficult than salting because the ingredients may be spoiled before the food is thoroughly dried. Furthermore, in China large high fences surrounded the yards, so no one could see the food drying in the backyard. In America it is more inconvenient to dry foods in open backyards and is not commonly done.

7. Smoking

The smoking method is just like rack steaming. The ingredients are placed on a rack in a pot lined with aluminum foil. An old pot is recommended to avoid the damage done to a new pot by smoking. Scatter brown sugar, ground anise, cinnamon or black tea leaves on the bottom of the rack. Cook over low heat covering the pot. The burning produces a thick strong smoke that chars the food and flavors it.

8. Cold-mixing

Ingredients such as vegetables can be parboiled, scalded or cooked before mixing with soy sauce, vinegar, sugar, pepper or hot pepper, and sesame oil (or salad oil). These dishes are cooled in the refrigerator and resemble American salad dishes.

V. CHINESE SERVING CUSTOMS

There are three kinds of dinners to mention here.

1. Family style meals

Several main dishes are placed in the center of the table for everyone to help oneself to a little of each. Each diner can see exactly how much food there is and pace himself accordingly. Rice is always served in individual bowls at each place setting. Once the food is served, the cook can remain seated like everyone else throughout the entire meal.

2. The company dinner

A company dinner usually consists of six or seven dishes and one soup for 6 to 8 people. It can be served the same way as the family style.

3. The formal banquets

A formal Chinese dinner for 10 or 12 people begins with four cold dishes (appetizers or hors d'oeuvres) and sometimes as many as six, followed by four stir-fried dishes and then four to six main courses such as Peking duck, a whole fish, and shark's fin dish. Soup such as bird's nest soup is always served after the main courses and desserts such as eight treasure rice pudding and sweet lotus seed soup are last. Wine is served throughout the meal. This is the traditional Chinese banquet. In present times the order of dishes is often changed, alternating stir-fried dishes with the main courses and soups. Champagne as well as wine can be served throughout the meal.

The number of servings of each recipe is found in the top right hand corner of each recipe. C stands for the number of servings for a Chinese style meal and W stands for the number of servings for a Western style meal. In other words, if a recipe states C: 4-6 servings, then that particular dish in combination with 4-6 other similarly designated recipes will serve 4-6 people, whereas W: 2-3 servings means that for 2-3 people, this dish will serve as the main course along with another dish with the same servings of food. The Chinese style of serving requires a number of varied dishes with small portions for each diner in contrast to the Western style, where there is usually one main course accented by a few side dishes. The recipes in this book have been adjusted to both styles of serving.

CONVERSION TABLE
BRITISH UNITS TO METRIC UNITS

British Unit	Metric Unit
1 ounce (oz.)	28.35 grams (gm.)
1 pound (lb.)	453.59 gm.
1 cup	236 cubic centimeters (c.c.)
1 tablespoon (tbsp.)	15 c.c. approximately
1 teaspoon (tsp.)	5 c.c. approximately
1 inch	2.54 centimeter (cm.)

2

TIPS AND
COMMON SENSE

This section on Tips and Common Sense of Chinese Cooking is the result of years of experimentation and experience (and should be referred to). The tips are divided into the following sections for easy reference: General, Stocks, Meat, Seafood, and Vegetables.

General:
1. Select the freshest and best quality of ingredients possible.
2. If the ingredient is tossed with egg white and cornstarch, coat it in warm oil once before cooking. This will make it more tender, smooth and attractive.
3. Freezing does not affect all foods the same. Some such as red meat and poultry are not affected as much as are some fish. Some frozen vegetables may have been picked younger and may be of more dependable quality than the fresh ones available during most seasons.
4. There are three kinds of rice; long grain, medium grain and short grain. The long grain is the type of grain used for cooking Chinese fried rice and is generally sold in the American market. The other two kinds of grain are available at most ordinary grocery stores. Accompanying main courses and for everyday use, medium grain rice is preferred.
5. Keep the chopping board clean. After chopping onions or other strong-flavored foods, always turn the chopping board over or wash it clean before slicing other ingredients.
6. Always heat the pan and oil very hot (until the oil is bubbling, not smoking). The oil should be thin and flowing before adding the ingredients, otherwise the ingredients will stick to the pan and be limp.
7. After deep frying, the oil can be saved and reused. If you reheat the oil, add 1 or 2 cups of potato slices and fry them for several minutes. Then drain the oil and discard the potato slices. The oil will be cleaner and less odorous.
8. If the number of servings in a recipe is not sufficient, the amount of ingredients can be increased according to need. The only exceptions are stir-fried recipes which cannot be doubled. If a greater quantity is needed, cook the recipe in two batches using separate pans or cooking one first and then the other.

9. Serving platters are better if put in a low-temperature oven to warm them. This will help the food stay warmer longer.
10. Fresh eggs have a rough texture on the shells. If shaken, there are no noises inside. When the egg is held up against the light, there should be no dark spots.

Stocks:

1. Stock is very important to Chinese cooking. There are meat stocks, chicken stocks or the mixture stocks of chicken bone and meat bone. The chicken stock (chicken broth) is the best for Chinese cooking.
2. How to make stock simply and cheaply? Use the chicken carcass, necks, or bones from the breast or legs. Chop a couple of pieces of ginger root. Pork bones can be used, but beef bones are not recommended because of their strong odor. Place the ingredients in a pot with water to cover. Bring to boil and reduce heat immediately. Skim off all the impurities on the surface. Cover and simmer 2 to 4 hours. Add salt when almost done. Then pour the stock through a strainer and discard the bones. Save the stock for cooking.
3. Substitute stock. Canned chicken broth or chicken bouillon powder or cubes are adequate substitutes.
4. Emergency stock. Use 1 tsp. monosodium glutamate, 1 cup of water, 1 tsp. soy sauce and a dash of pepper.
5. To obtain clear broths or stocks, skim off the impurities rising to the surface when the stock boils. Turn heat to low and simmer or skim the fat off the stock after refrigeration.

Meats:

1. Choice of fresh meat. If you can get fresh meat, the color of fresh pork should be light red and its fat part should be fine, smooth and white. The color of fresh beef should be bright red and its fat part should be milk white and elastic.
2. For Chinese cooking, the ingredients are always cut into neat slices, shreds, cubes or dices. If the meat (pork, beef, poultry) is partially frozen, it will be easier to cut.
3. The meat will taste much better and more tender if you cut the meat (pork, beef, poultry) against or across the grain, that is, perpendicular to the direction of the fibers.
4. Before cooking a duck, discard the tail end including the oil pouches because it has strong odor and lots of fat.
5. To cut poultry (chicken and duck) into medium-sized pieces, use a heavy cleaver to chop off the head if there is any. Cut off the neck, and then cut the neck into 2 or 3 sections. Clip off the legs, then cut each leg into 3 or 4 sections. Clip off the wings close to the body; then cut each wing into 2 sections. Lay the fowl on its back, breast side up, and cut it in two down the center of the breast by using a rubber mallet to pound the cleaver

through the bone. With the aid of the rubber mallet, cut each half into halves again. Each of the four long strips are further cut into 1½-2 inch chunks.

6. Before cooking meat and seafood, mix with some cornstarch so that the meat will taste more tender.

7. Choice of kidneys and livers. The color of liver should be light purple-red and the color of kidney should be dark red and not white. If you press down on the meat, water should not come out.

Seafood:

1. Shrimp is cooked with or without the shells according to the recipe used. It is important to remove the dark gritty line along the back, otherwise it will have a bad smell and taste. In order to prevent cooked shrimp from curving, before cooking pull away or cut off the white vein from the stomach.

2. Buy fish which has never been frozen, if possible (although this is becoming increasingly difficult). Learn to look at a fish in the eyes and gills. The eyes should be firm, clear and bright. The gills should be reddish inside. A whole fish should look firm with no trace of shrinking whether fresh or frozen and thawed. Whenever fish has been cut, the pieces should be moist and lively in color—fresh looking.

3. It is hard to get fresh seafood such as shrimps, scallops, lobsters, clams, crabs and oysters. (Sometimes fresh clams, crabs and lobsters can be found in seafood shops.) However, even if you can only buy frozen seafood, be sure the frozen product is solidly frozen and has no sign of having been partially thawed and refrozen or having been frozen too long.

4. Steam or cook seafood. To get the best flavor and tenderness, wait for the water to boil, then add the seafood to the pot or steamer.

5. In order to cook a live fish, use the back of knife or a mallet to hit its head. When it is unconscious, cut and scrape it.

6. In preparing live crabs, wash and clean them; then use a sharp stick to prick the hearts before cooking. When they die, cook immediately.

7. How to cut lobsters: Lay lobsters on a cutting board. Cut each body lengthwise in two, then across into 1½ inch-long sections. Chop each head into 4 parts and each claw into 3 sections. Discard legs, intestines, sacs in the tip of the head, and the spongy gills. Crush the arm shells for easy eating. If cutting a live lobster bothers you, first plunge the lobster in boiling water or steam for a minute.

8. Ginger and sherry will neutralize the fishy flavor of seafood.

Vegetables:

1. To get the best quality in vegetables and fruits, try to take advantage of those which are at the peak of their season. These have fuller flavor, more natural color and firmer texture when cooked.

2. In order to keep the color of fresh green vegetables, stir-fry in hot oil in the pan or pot. Sprinkle salt on the vegetables. Do not cover, and stir constantly until the vegetables are crisp or crunchy. Spread on the serving plate and serve immediately.
3. If the dried black fermented beans seem to be drying out, just add a few drops of vegetable oil and the beans will then be all right.
4. When dicing irregularly shaped vegetables, begin at the narrowest section and work toward the thickest.
5. Before cooking dried bean curd, soak in hot water with some baking soda. It will speed the softening process of the bean curd.
6. If you have frozen snow pea pods, wash them in cold water and drain before you cook them.
7. When shredding ginger, follow the pattern of the fibers which run vertically down the roots.
8. For canned bean sprouts, rinse with cold water and soak them in ice water several hours before using. This will improve the crispness.
9. In order to retain the crunchiness and tenderness of vegetables, add to hot oil and season immediately.
10. Place vegetables on a large platter because crowding food speeds up color deterioration from the heating process.

3

MENU PLANNING

In planning a menu we must remember the following points:
1. The texture of each dish should be varied.
2. Each main ingredient should not appear twice on the same menu.
3. The color combination should be attractive.
4. Variation in taste of each dish should be taken into consideration.
Chinese serving customs are described in Chapter I.

The Chinese place setting: Each setting includes a soup bowl set on a plate. A pair of chopsticks is to the right of the plate; to the right of the chopsticks, a teacup. If a second bowl is used, it is placed to the upper left. If an individual dip dish is used, it is placed at the upper center. If a wine cup is used, it is at the upper right, next to the teacup (handleless porcelain cup).

In general, the seat at the inner side of the room facing the entrance is for the guest of honor, while the seats on the serving side are for the host and hostess. The guest of honor is always facing the host.

In western style, we always serve a main course with several side dishes. If the number of servings in a recipe is not sufficient, the amount of ingredients can be increased according to need. The only exceptions are stir-fried recipes which can not be doubled. If a greater quantity is needed, cook the recipe in two or more batches using separate pans or cooking one first and then the others.

How to use the chopsticks: Chopsticks are always used in pairs for eating. Although the two are alike, each differs in function. One is stationary; the other one moves. To understand their functions, rest the upper half of the stationary stick on the juncture of your thumb and index fingers, and the lower half on the end of the ring finger. Use the thumb, index and middle fingers to hold the moving stick. The right place to put your fingers is roughly at the middle of the chopsticks. The stationary one is in the lower position, while the moving one  is in upper position which moves freely as you wish. Your little finger is used to support the ring finger.

The following menus are to give an idea of the different combinations of taste, texture and the type of dishes that are desired. Recipes for two can be doubled for four servings (see the above section on stir-fry dishes) and so on. Two formal banquet dinners are included for completeness.

A. Menus for 2

Cold eggplant
Sour and sweet pork
Boiled rice
Fresh fruits and tea

Chicken vermicelli soup
Red cooked beef
Steamed rolls or fancy rolls
Fresh fruits and tea

Egg drop soup
Beef with green peppers
Boiled rice
Almond cookies or fruits and tea

Egg rolls
Sour and sweet pork
Boiled rice
Fresh fruits or jelled almond fruit
    dessert and tea

Egg rolls or stir-fried dandelion
Moo-shi meat
Chinese pancakes
Fresh fruits or jelled almond fruit
    dessert and tea

Egg drop soup
Pork strips and broccoli stems
    with noodles
Jellied chicken
Fortune cookies, fruits and tea

Wonton soup
Broccoli with beef
Boiled rice or steamed buns
Fortune cookies or fruits and tea

Watercress soup
Beef in oyster sauce
Boiled rice
Almond cookies or fruits and tea

Cold asparagus
Sour and sweet pork
Boiled rice
Fresh fruits or almond
    cookies and tea

Sour and hot soup
Roast pork I
Steamed rolls and fancy rolls
Fresh fruits or jelled almond fruit
    dessert and tea

B. Menus for 4

Cold asparagus
Steamed whiting fish
Sauteed pork with scallions
Diced chicken and green peppers
Boiled rice
Ice cream and tea

Wonton soup
Sour and sweet pork
Cold asparagus
Jellied chicken
Boiled rice
Fresh fruits and tea

Egg rolls
Moo-shi meat
Chinese pancakes
Broccoli with beef
Flavored steam chicken
Fresh fruits and tea

Cold asparagus
Steamed whiting fish
Boiled rice
Tomato with bean curd
    (or sweet onions with beef shreds)
Fresh fruits and tea

Chicken vermicelli soup
Cold cucumbers
Peking duck
Chinese pancakes
Broccoli with beef
Fresh fruits, almond cookies and tea

Watercress soup
Roast spareribs
Celery cabbage in chicken sauce
Shrimp with peas
Boiled rice
Jelled almond fruit dessert and tea

C. Menus for 6

Breaded shrimp rolls
Egg drop soup
Sour and sweet pork
Broccoli with beef
Diced chicken and green peppers
Boiled rice
Jelled almond fruit dessert and tea

Egg rolls
Moo-shi meat
Chinese pancakes
Bean curd with beef and hot sauce
Stir-fry shrimp curls
Salted chicken
Boiled rice or steamed rolls
Fresh fruits, fortune cookies and tea

Shrimp toast
Party chicken
Pork with hot peppers
Red cooked beef
Cold asparagus
Boiled rice
Almond cookies or fresh fruits and tea

Winter melon soup
Peking duck or roast duck
Chinese pancakes
Stuffed cucumbers
Splashed shrimp
Cauliflower with water chestnuts
Boiled rice
Almond cookies and tea

D. Menus for 8

Egg drop soup
Beef with American cabbage
Red cooked fish
Ground pork with bean curd
Salted chicken
Cauliflower with water chestnuts
Boiled rice
Jelled almond fruit dessert and tea

Egg rolls
Chicken vermicelli soup
Sour and sweet pork
Broccoli with beef
Cold asparagus
Shrimp with ketchup
Boiled rice
Fresh fruits and tea

Fried dumplings (Kuo-Tieh)
Egg Foo Yung
Red cooked beef
Pork shreds with onions
Steamed fillet haddock
Stir-fry broccoli cup
Boiled rice or steamed rolls
Fortune cookies and tea

Watercress soup
Egg rolls
Red cooked spareribs
Shrimp with ketchup
Diced chicken with green peppers
Broccoli with beef
Boiled rice
Eight treasure rice pudding and tea

Sour and hot soup
Roast beef II
Cold asparagus
Pork strips with leeks and bean sprouts
Shrimp with peas
Chicken cubelet
Boiled rice
Jelled almond fruit dessert and tea

E. Menus for 10 to 12

Egg rolls
Lion heads
Red cooked chicken
Shrimp with ketchup
Stir-fry broccoli cup
Sweet onions with beef shreds
Roast pork and egg rice
Steamed rolls
Eight treasure rice pudding and tea

Breaded shrimp rolls
Beef with green peppers
Egg dumplings
Flavored steamed chicken
Butterfly shrimp
Cold asparagus
Red cooked duck
Boiled rice
Eight jewel congee or ice cream and tea

Winter melon soup or wonton soup
Red cooked shoulder ham
Party chicken
Glutinous rice balls
Beef with American cabbage
Shrimp with peas
Yang Chow fried rice
Steamed rolls
Fresh fruits, fortune cookies and tea

Fried dumplings (Kuo-Tieh)
Roast pork II
Pork and bean curd, home style
Stir-fry shrimp curls
Chicken casserole
Pork strips and broccoli stems with noodles
Cauliflower with water chestnuts
Boiled rice
Fresh fruits and tea

F. Chinese Banquet (Menus for 10 to 12)

I. Appetizers, served simultaneously:

Salted chicken	Stir-fry shrimp curls
Red cooked beef	Cold asparagus

Four fried dishes, served one at a time:

Beef with vermicelli
Sauteed pork with scallions
Shrimp with peas
Pork with bean curd, home style

Six main courses with boiled rice:

Chicken cubelets or paper wrapped chicken
Sour and sweet pork
Peking duck and Chinese pancakes or crispy duck
Stir-fry lobsters, Cantonese style
Moo-shi meat and Chinese pancakes
Red cooked fish

Soup: Shark fin soup

Dessert: Eight treasure rice pudding
Jelled almond fruit dessert
Tea

II. Appetizers, served simultaneously:

Jellied chicken	Cold asparagus
sweet ham	Red cooked chicken livers

Four fried dishes, served one at a time:

Stir-fry shrimp curls
Diced chicken with peppers
Pork with hot peppers
Broccoli with beef

Four main courses, served one at a time:

Peking duck with Chinese pancakes
Butterfly shrimp
Paper wrapped chicken
Steamed whiting fish

Soup: Winter melon soup (whole)

Dessert: Eight treasure rice pudding
Jelled almond fruit dessert
Tea

中國烹飪

熊余文琴 著

4

APPETIZERS
AND SOUPS

C: 4-5 Servings
W: 4 Servings

蛋花湯

EGG DROP SOUP

2 eggs
1½ tsp. sherry

(a) 1 cup cold water
2 cups chicken broth (fresh
or canned)
½ tsp. salt or salt to taste
2 slices ginger root (if ob-
tainable)

(b) 2 tbsp. cornstarch
2 tbsp. water

1 scallion, chopped
2 tbsp. minced water chestnut
¼ tsp. monosodium glutamate
(optional)

1. Beat the eggs with sherry very well.

2. Boil the ingredients (a) in a sauce pan over medium high heat. When the soup boils, turn to low heat and simmer about 5 minutes. Then discard the ginger roots. Turn to medium high heat. When the soup boils again, pour the egg mixture slowly into the soup. Keep stirring the soup while pouring the egg mixture. Then add the ingredients (b) into the soup. Stir constantly until thickened. Add the monosodium glutamate and stir well.

3. Pour into individual serving bowls. Garnish with minced scallions and water chestnuts. Serve hot.

NOTE: The soup can also be garnished with scallions and water chestnuts before pouring into the individual bowls.

酸辣湯

SOUR AND HOT SOUP

4 oz. shredded pork
4 dried mushrooms
20 tiger lily stems
¼ cup wood ears
1 square bean curd (shredded)
¼ cup shredded bamboo shoots

(a) 1 tsp. sherry
     1 tsp. cornstarch

(b) 1 tbsp. soy sauce
     2 cups chicken broth or
       stock
     2 cups water
     1 tsp. salt
     1 tsp. sugar
     ¼ tsp. monosodium gluta-
       mate (optional)

(c) 3 tsp. white vinegar
     1 tsp. white or black pepper

(d) 2½ tbsp. cornstarch
     3 tbsp. water

(e) 1 tsp. sesame oil
     1½ tbsp. minced scallions

1 egg, beaten

1. Mix the pork shreds with ingredients (a). Let stand in the refrigerator for ½ hour.

2. Place the mushrooms, tiger lily stems and wood ears in separate bowls. Pour boiling water over them and let stand 15-20 minutes. Cut off the stems of the mushrooms and cut the mushrooms into slices. Cut tiger lily stems into halves if too long. Break wood ears into small pieces if too big. Set aside.

3. Boil seasonings (b) in a large sauce pan over medium high heat. After boiling, add the mixed pork and stir quickly. Cook until boiling again, add the mushrooms, tiger lily stems, wood ears, and bamboo shoots. Stir

thoroughly. When the soup boils again, add the bean curd and seasonings (c) and stir well. Then pour the beaten egg slowly into the soup. Keep stirring the soup while pouring the egg. Add the blending mixture (d) and stir until the soup thickens.

4. Pour the hot soup into a serving bowl. Add the seasonings (e). Stir well and serve hot.

水田芥湯

WATERCRESS SOUP

2 bunches of fresh watercress
6 dried black mushrooms
1 bamboo shoot (from a can)
1 tsp. monosodium glutamate (optional)
6-8 cups chicken broth or stock
½ tsp. salt (salt to taste)

1. Soak mushrooms in boiling water about 15-20 minutes. Drain and squeeze to remove excess moisture. Cut off and discard the tough stem. Shred the caps. Set aside.

2. Wash the bamboo shoot and cut into shreds.

3. Trim off and discard the tougher parts of the watercress stems, leaving those that are tender. Rinse the watercress well and shake or pat dry (There should be about 7 or 8 cups of loosely packed leaves with tender stems).

4. Pour the chicken broth into a deep pot. Bring the broth to a boil over medium high heat. Add the salt, bamboo shoot, and mushrooms. Cook about ½ minute. Add the watercress and the monosodium glutamate. Stir, then turn off the heat. Let stand about 5-10 minutes and serve (If using an electric stove, just turn off the heat. The heat gradually cools down. If using a gas stove, leave the heat on about 1 minute and then turn it off).

蝦吐司

SHRIMP TOAST

8 oz. raw shrimp, shelled and deveined
1-2 oz. pork suet

(a) 1 egg white
   salt to taste
   ½ tsp. monosodium glutamate (optional)
   2 tsp. cornstarch
   ¼ cup baked ham (Smithfield is best, but not necessary)
   1 tsp. sherry

¼ tsp. parsley chopped

(b) 1 egg white
   salt to taste
   1 tbsp. cornstarch

(c) 1 egg yolk
   1 tsp. cornstarch

7-8 slices of white bread
4 cups vegetable or corn oil

1. Chop the suet into pieces. Using an electric blender at low speed, blend shrimp, suet pieces, and ingredients (a) into a paste. Spoon and scrape into mixing bowl. Stir in chopped parsley.

2. Trim away the crusts from the bread slices. Cut each slice diagonally into 4 triangles.

3. Mix ingredients (b) in a bowl. Brush one side of each triangle with the cornstarch mixture (b). Spoon equal amounts of the shrimp paste onto the triangle of bread (on the cornstarch-brushed side) very evenly.

4. Blend ingredients (c) and brush it onto the side of the triangle of bread without the shrimp paste.

26

5. Heat the oil in the deep fryer (350°F) or in a frying pan (until a piece of bread forms bubbles). Add the triangle pieces of bread, keeping the shrimp side up. Let the triangles cook gently in the oil over medium heat. After 2-3 minutes, turn the pieces of bread over and cook 6-8 minutes longer, or until golden brown. Drain on paper towels and serve immediately while still hot.

茶葉蛋

TEA EGGS

2 dozen eggs

(a) ½ cup black tea leaves
     ¼ tsp. five spice powder
     2 tbsp. salt
     1 tsp. monosodium gluta-
        mate (optional)
     1 tsp. sugar

1. Put the eggs in a big pot over medium heat. When the water boils, reduce to low heat. Simmer about one hour. Let cool and drain. (Do not boil the eggs over high heat; otherwise, the shells will break.)

2. Crack the egg shells all over but do not peel from the eggs.

3. Add enough water to cover the eggs and boil over medium high heat. Add ingredients (a) and mix well. When the sauce boils turn to low heat. Simmer another 1 to 2 hours. Turn off the heat and let the eggs stand in the sauce at least overnight.

4. Drain and peel the shells. Cut into 6 wedges and serve.

NOTE: The eggs can be kept at room temperature for a few days. If the eggs get too salty, they can be desalted by soaking in fresh water.

炸雲吞

FRIED WONTON

Skin:

Buy a pound of wonton skin (already made) in Chinese grocery. If you can not get it you can make it as follows:

(a) 1 egg
1¾ to 2 cups flour
1 tsp. salt
½ cup cornstarch
½ to ¾ cup water

1. Mix ingredients (a) in a large bowl and knead until very smooth. Cover the dough with a damp cloth. Refrigerate ½ hour to 1 hour.

2. Sprinkle a board with flour. With a rolling pin (rub the rolling pin with flour to prevent sticking), roll out the dough again and again (in a forward motion away from you) until it is paper thin and its edges are even in thickness. Cut into 3-inch squares to make wonton skin. Rub flour evenly on each skin before stacking to prevent sticking together. Wrap the wonton skins in aluminum foil or a plastic bag and store in refrigerator until ready to use. This will make about 45-50 skins.

Filling:

½ lb. lean ground pork
¼ lb. shelled and deveined shrimp

(a) 1 egg
2 tbsp. scallions, chopped fine
1 cup celery cabbage leaves, chopped fine
2 tbsp. soy sauce
¼ tsp. ginger root, chopped fine, or ⅛ tsp. ginger powder
1 tsp. salt or salt to taste
1 tbsp. sherry
3 tbsp. water
1 tsp. cornstarch
½ tsp. sesame oil

4 cups vegetable oil

3. Chop the shrimp into fine pieces. Mix the pork, shrimp and the ingredients (a) very well. Let stand about 15 to 30 minutes. Place about 1 level teaspoon of filling slightly below center of the skin. Moisten the two adjacent edges of the skin with water. Fold the skin diagonally in half to form a triangle. Press the edges to seal. Moisten the front of the triangle's right corner and the back of the left corner. With a twisting action, bring the two moistened surfaces together and pinch to seal, as shown in the picture.

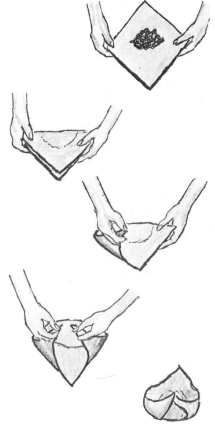

(1)

Place about 1 tsp. filling slightly below the center of the skin.

(2)

Fold the skin diagonally in half to form a triangle. Press the edges to seal.

(3)

Overlap the tip of the right corner toward the center.

(4)

Moisten the front of the tip of the right corner and the back of the tip of the left corner. With a twisting action pinch them together.

(5)

This is the finished wonton.

4. Use a deep fryer or a deep pan. Pour in 4 cups of oil over medium high heat. When the oil is hot, drop the wonton into the oil (about 10 at a time). Reduce the heat to medium. Fry them about 4-5 minutes or until golden brown and crispy. Drain on paper towels. Serve hot.

BREADED SHRIMP ROLL

1 package of white bread
1 lb. shrimp, shelled and deveined
6 oz. pork fat (white fat)

(a)　　　**dash ginger powder (about
　　　　¼ tsp.)
　　　　dash black pepper (about
　　　　¼ tsp.)**
　　¾ tsp. salt or salt to taste
　　1 tbsp. sherry
　　¼ tsp. sesame oil
　　1 tsp. monosodium gluta-
　　　　mate (optional)

(b)　　　**flour
　　　　water
　　　　mix it as a paste mixture.**

4 cups of vegetable oil

1. Grind the shrimp and fat with knife. Mix it with ingredients (a) very well. Let stand in the refrigerator for ½ hour to 1 hour.

2. Remove the crust from the bread. Roll each slice of bread into very thin skin. Cover and set aside. Repeat until all the pieces of bread have been rolled into very thin skins.

3. Put 1 to 2 tbsp. of shrimp filling into one side of each skin. Roll it. Brush the side and both ends with the flour mixture. Push and pinch them very tightly, as illustrated below:

Put the filling on the skin.

Press it very tight.

4. Heat the vegetable oil in a deep pot, over medium high heat, or a deep fryer. When the oil is very hot (drop a piece of bread; when there are bubbles, the temperature is then right) or 375°F in a fryer; reduce the heat to medium. Put the rolls into the oil lightly. Fry them until light brown. Serve hot.

NOTE:　The rolls can be frozen. When needed, put the frozen rolls in the oven at about 325°F to 350°F for about 10-20 minutes.

30

冬瓜湯

WINTER MELON SOUP

(a) 1 lb. winter melon
   4-5 dried Chinese mushrooms
      (1 to 1½ inches diameter)
   3 cups chicken broth (fresh
      or canned)
   ¼ tsp. salt (salt to taste)

¼ lb. lean pork slices or cooked
   ham (Smithfield preferred), ¼
   inch thick slice cut into 1-inch
   squares

(b) ¼ tsp. salt
   1 tsp. cornstarch

1. Soak the dry Chinese mushrooms in boiling water for 15 minutes. Drain and cut away the stems of the mushrooms. Cut each cap into dices.

2. If you use fresh pork slices, mix the meat slices with ingredients (b). Let stand about ½ hour in the refrigerator.

3. Peel off the skin of melon and discard the inner seeds and stringy fibers. Cut the melon into ¼ inch slices and then cut the slices into 1-inch squares.

4. Put ingredients (a) in a large saucepan. Bring to a boil. Reduce to low heat and partially cover the pan. Simmer about 10-15 minutes until the melon is tender.

5. If fresh lean pork slices are used, simmer the soup another 7-8 minutes and then add the pork. Simmer 3-4 minutes more.

6. If cooked ham dices are used, wait for the soup to be done then ladle the soup into a serving bowl and garnish with the ham squares. Serve immediately while hot.

冬瓜盅

WINTER MELON SOUP (Whole)

9-10 lbs. winter melon

(a) ¼ cup diced Smithfield ham
     ¼ cup diced lean pork
     ¼ cup diced fresh mushroom
     1 large chicken breast, diced
     2 oz. fresh shrimp, shelled
       and deveined
     ½ cup cooked lotus seeds or
       ¼ cup blanched almonds
   5-6 cups chicken broth
     ½ tsp. salt or salt to taste
       dash of black or white
       pepper
     1 tbsp. chicken fat (optional)
     6 dried mushrooms, about 1
       to 1½ inch diameter

cornstarch
salt
sherry

1. Buy a nice round and circular cylinder winter melon. Wash and wipe it
   clean. Cut the top off from the root end of the melon. Scoop out all the
   seeds and fibers. Sprinkle ½ tsp. salt over the top and the inside wall of the
   melon. Place melon in a deep heatproof bowl. Stand on a rack in a steamer
   or a big pot filled with 2 or 3 inches boiling water over medium high heat.
   When the water boils, turn to medium heat. Cover and cook the melon
   about 4-5 hours or until tender.

2. Soak the dried mushrooms in boiling water for 15 to 20 minutes. Squeeze
   off the water from the mushrooms. Cut away and discard the tough stems
   and cut each cap into 4 quarters. Set aside.

3. Bone the chicken breasts. Remove the gristle and fiber from the meat. Cut
   against the grain into strips, then cut each strip into dices. Rub ¼ tsp. salt
   and ½ tsp. cornstarch with the chicken meat. Set aside.

4. If the shrimp is of large or medium size, cut into small pieces. Rub with ½
   tsp. sherry, ¼ tsp. salt, and ¼ tsp. cornstarch. Set aside.

5. Mix the diced lean pork with ¼ tsp. salt and ½ tsp. cornstarch. Set aside.

6. After the winter melon is tender, heat the 6 cups chicken broth in a big pot over medium high heat. When the soup boils add ingredients (a) and stir and mix well until the mixture boils again. Spoon the mixture into the cavity of the winter melon. (If the melon can not hold the entire soup mixture, just leave the soup mixture in the pot for later replenishing of the melon when serving.) Cover the steamer. When the water boils turn to low heat. Steam another ½ hour.

7. To serve: Leave the melon standing in bowl. After serving the soup in the melon, cut pieces of melon carefully along the edge of the cavity and add to the soup mixture. (Do not break the skin.)

NOTE: Watermelon may substitute for winter melon. Cut as directed above; remove seeds and scoop out enough melon pulp to leave a 2-inch thick melon shell.

魚翅湯

SHARK'S FIN SOUP

2 oz. precooked and cleaned shark's fin

(a) 2 scallions, cut in half
     2 sliced ginger roots
     2 tbsp. sherry
1 chicken breast

(b) 5 dried Chinese mushrooms
     ½ cup bamboo shoots, cooked and shredded
     ½ tsp. monosodium glutamate (optional)
     ½ tsp. salt, or salt to taste
     ½ tsp. sugar

2 tbsp. cooked ham, shredded (Smithfield ham preferred)

(c) 2 tbsp. cornstarch
     2 tbsp. water

4 cups chicken broth
Dash of black pepper

1. Soak the shark's fin in the cold water for 8-10 hours or overnight. Drain off the water and divide it into small pieces if it is too big. Put the shark's fin and ingredients (a) in a pot with fresh water over medium high heat. When the water boils, reduce the heat to low and cook uncovered for ½ hour. Drain and discard water, scallions and ginger. Rinse under cold running water. Drain again and set aside.

2. Cook the chicken breast with ½ tsp. salt and water over medium high heat. When the water boils, turn to low heat. Cover and simmer about 15-20 minutes. After the meat is tender, take out the chicken breast. Save the chicken broth for another use. Bone and skin the chicken breast. Cut the meat into shreds. Set aside.

3. Soak the mushrooms in boiling water for 15-20 minutes. Cut off the hard tough stems of the mushrooms. Cut the caps of the mushrooms into slices, then cut into shreds. Set aside.

4. Pour the 4 cups chicken broth into a deep pot over medium high heat. Add the shark's fin, chicken and ingredients (b). When the soup boils, reduce to low heat and simmer for a few minutes. If not salty enough, salt to taste. Turn heat to medium high heat. When the soup starts to boil, pour the paste ingredients (c) into it. Stir constantly until thickened.

5. Pour the soup into a big bowl. Sprinkle with ham shreds and black pepper. Serve hot.

2058850

C: 6-8 Servings
W: 4-6 Servings

粉絲湯

CHICKEN VERMICELLI SOUP

¼ lb. packet vermicelli (bean thread)
4 cups chicken broth or stock
2 cups of water

(a) 1 tsp. salt
2 tbsp. sherry
½ tsp. monosodium glutamate (optional)

(b) 4 tbsp. shredded cooked chicken
2 tbsp. shredded ham (Smithfield preferred)
2 scallions, minced

1. Use scissors to cut the vermicelli into 4 or 5-inch sections. Soak in a bowl with boiling water for several hours.

2. Heat up the chicken broth and water in a saucepan over medium high heat. Add ingredients (a). When the soup boils, turn to medium heat and add the vermicelli. Cook a few minutes and if it is not salty enough, salt to taste.

3. Pour the soup and vermicelli into six or eight bowls. Garnish with ingredients (b). Serve hot.

WONTON SOUP

The skin can be made as the fried wonton skin recipe (see index), or you can buy them from a Chinese grocery. You can also buy egg roll skin and cut it into 4 equal portions (the skin is the same and cheaper when bought in egg roll skin quantities).

For the filling:

½ lb. ground pork
¼ lb. shelled and deveined
    shrimp, chopped

(a)   1 egg
      2 tbsp. chopped scallions
      1 cup celery cabbage leaves,
        chopped fine
      2 tbsp. soy sauce
      ¼ tsp. ginger root, chopped
        fine
      1 tsp. salt or salt to taste
      1 tsp. sherry
      3 tbsp. water
      1 tsp. cornstarch
      ½ tsp. sesame oil

2 tbsp. chopped scallions
2 tbsp. diced Szechuan preserved
    cabbage (if obtainable)
some small slices roast pork
some watercress or spinach

1. Mix the pork, shrimp and ingredients (a) very well. Let stand ½ to 1 hour. Place about 1½ to 2 tsp. filling in the center of the skin. Moisten the edges of the skin with water. Fold the skin in half to form a rectangle. Press the edges to seal. Moisten the front of the rectangular right corner and the back of the left corner. With a twisting action, bring the two moistened surfaces together and pinch to seal (shown in the picture). Makes 50-60 wontons.

2. Drop wonton into deep pot of boiling water over medium high heat (add them gradually so as not to lower the temperature abruptly). Cover with lid and cook several seconds over medium high heat. When water boils again, add ½ cup of cold water, let boil up one more time until the wonton floats (about 5-8 minutes). Remove with a slotted spoon into the serving bowls.

3. Meanwhile, cook chicken broth in another pot. When it boils, pour over the wonton. Garnish with scallions, roast pork, diced Szechuan preserved cabbage, watercress or spinach (or a combination of the above ingredients).

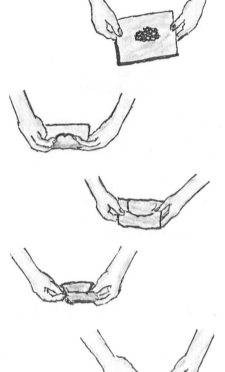

(1)

Place about 1½ to 2 teaspoonfuls of filling straight across the skin.

(2)

Fold one side of the skin over the filling. Moisten the edges of the skin with water.

(3)

Fold the skin in half to form a rectangle.

(4)

Press the edge to seal.

(5)

Moisten the front of the right corner and back of the left corner. With a twisting action, bring the two moistened surfaces together and pinch to seal.

NOTES: 1. The wonton can be steamed in a steamer. Place the wonton one layer deep in a slightly oiled heat proof platter. Allow enough space between them so they will not stick together. Steam 10-15 minutes.

2. The cold cooked wonton can be braised as fried wonton. Heat 2 tbsp. oil, add wonton and brown quickly on both sides. Add ¼ cup stock or water and bring to boil. Then reduce heat and cook covered until done (3-5 minutes).

榨菜粉絲湯

SZECHUAN PRESERVED CABBAGE AND VERMICELLI SOUP

2 oz. pork loin (boneless), sliced

(a)   1 tbsp. soy sauce
      1½ tsp. cornstarch

(b)   4 cups chicken broth or water
      1 tsp. salt or salt to taste
      1 tsp. monosodium glutamate (optional)

¼ cup thinly sliced Szechuan preserved cabbage
½ cup thinly sliced cucumber

(c)   1 tbsp. chopped scallions
      ¼ tsp. black pepper
      ½ tsp. sesame oil
      1 tsp. soy sauce

2 oz. vermicelli

1. Partially freeze the meat. Cut the meat against the grain into thin slices. Mix with ingredients (a) and let stand for ½ hour.

2. Use scissors to cut the vermicelli into 4- or 5-inch sections. Soak the vermicelli for several hours in a bowl of hot water.

3. Rinse the preserved cabbage well under running water and pat dry with paper towels. Cut it into thin slices.

4. Bring ingredients (b) to boil. Add the vermicelli, meat, Szechuan preserved cabbage and cucumber. Cook for several minutes.

5. Place ingredients (c) in a large serving bowl. Pour the soup over it and serve hot.

5

BEEF

烤牛排

CHINESE MARINATED STEAK

2 lb. porterhouse steak (½-inch thickness), T-bone steak (½-inch thickness) or beef tenderloin

(a)   **4 tbsp. soy sauce**
    ½ tsp. ginger powder
    ½ tsp. garlic powder
    ¼ cup chicken broth
    ½ tsp. salt or salt to taste
    ½ tsp. monosodium glutamate (optional)

1. If you use beef tenderloin, cut it against the grain into ⅓-inch thick slices.

2. Marinate the beef in ingredients (a). Soak for several hours or overnight, at least one or two hours.

3. Set the oven for 300°F and put the steak on the pan about 2 or 3 inches from the broiler. Broil each side of the steak about 4 to 8 minutes depending upon whether you like rare, medium or well done. If the temperature of your oven cannot be adjusted on broil, you can adjust the rack's distance from the broiler.

NOTE: 1. In the summer, this is a good picnic dish. You can cook the steaks on the grating of a charcoal grill or any other kind of grill (gas or electric).

      2. If you prefer, you can also fry the steaks on both sides in 2 tbsp. vegetable oil in a frying pan over high heat for a total of 3 or 4 minutes or until done to taste.

捲心菜炒牛肉絲

C: 5-6 Servings
W: 4 Servings

BEEF WITH AMERICAN CABBAGE

½ lb. flank steak
1 cabbage (about 1 lb.)
(a) 2 tbsp. soy sauce
    1 tsp. sherry
    1 tsp. sugar
    ½ tsp. sesame oil (optional)
      or 1 tsp. vegetable oil
      dash ginger powder
      dash garlic powder
    1 tbsp. cornstarch

(b) 1 tsp. salt or salt to taste
    ½ tsp. monosodium gluta-
      mate (optional)
    ¼ cup chicken broth
    1 tsp. sherry

4 tbsp. vegetable oil

1. Cut the beef against the grain into slices, then shreds. (This is easier to cut if the meat is partially frozen.) Mix the beef shreds with ingredients (a). Toss them well. Let stand in the refrigerator or a cold place at least ½ hour.

2. Wash and cut the cabbage into thin shreds (similar to coleslaw).

3. Heat 3 tbsp. oil in a frying pan over medium high heat. When the oil is hot, add the beef. Stir quickly, about ½ to 1 minute, and separate the shreds. When the meat changes color, remove the beef and leave the oil, if any, in the pan.

4. Add the remaining 1 tbsp. oil over medium high heat. When the oil is hot, add the cabbage shreds and cook about ½ minute. Add ingredients (b), stir and cook about 3 or 4 minutes. Return the beef to the pan, stir thoroughly and cook about 1 or 2 minutes. (If not salty enough, salt to taste.) Serve hot.

NOTE: American cabbage can be substituted by bean sprouts, celery cabbage or string beans.

龍鬚菜炒牛肉
ASPARAGUS WITH BEEF

½ lb. flank steak or tenderloin
  beef
1 lb. asparagus

(a) 2 tsp. soy sauce
     1 tbsp. sherry
     1 tbsp. vegetable oil
     1 tsp. sugar
     2 tsp. cornstarch

(b) 1 tbsp. sherry
     ½ tsp. salt or to taste
     ½ tsp. monosodium gluta-
       mate (optional)
     2 tbsp. chicken broth

1 qt. boiling water
6 tbsp. vegetable or corn oil

1. Cut the partially frozen beef into slices and then cut into strips. Marinate the beef strips with ingredients (a). Mix well and let stand at least ½ hour in the refrigerator.

2. Break off the tough part of the asparagus near the root. Scrape with a swivel-bladed paring knife leaving the tips intact. Cut into long rolling-knife (see chapter 1) pieces of 1½-inch length. Wash and rinse them well. Put all the asparagus in a pot containing 1 qt. of boiling water. Bring the water to a boil again for about 2 minutes depending on the age and the size of the asparagus. Drain and immediately chill under cold running water. Drain well and set aside (you can keep the asparagus in the refrigerator if it is not for immediate use).

3. Heat 4 tbsp. oil in a frying pan over medium high heat. When the oil is hot, add the beef strips. Stir quickly about ½ minute (be sure to separate the beef strips). Remove the meat and leave the oil, if any, in the pan.

4. Add the remaining 2 tbsp. oil into the pan over medium high heat. When the oil is hot, add the asparagus. Stir for 10-20 seconds. Add ingredients (b). Stir for a few seconds. Return the beef strips. Stir thoroughly until almost all the sauce is absorbed into the beef. Serve hot.

蒲蘿克炒牛肉

BROCCOLI WITH BEEF

1 lb. flank steak or round steak

(a) 3 tbsp. soy sauce
1 tbsp. cornstarch
1 tsp. sugar
½ tsp. sesame oil or 1 tbsp. oil
1 tbsp. sherry

1 bunch of broccoli

(b) ½ tsp. salt or salt to taste
½ tsp. monosodium gluta- mate (optional)
1 tsp. sugar

6 tbsp. vegetable oil, peanut oil, or corn oil

1. Trim off the fat and gristle from the beef and slice the beef against the grain into slivers. Marinate the beef slivers with ingredients (a). Toss to coat thoroughly and let stand in the refrigerator at least half an hour.

2. Break the tops of the broccoli into "flowerets." If necessary, peel off the stems of the flowerets to make them more tender. Save the main broccoli stalks for other use (such as Pork Strips and Broccoli Stems).

3. Heat 2 tbsp. oil in a frying pan over medium high heat. When the oil is hot, add the broccoli. Stir a few seconds. Add ingredients (b). Stir thoroughly and cook about 1 minute until the broccoli is crunchy. Spoon out and drain. Place the broccoli on a warm serving platter in a warm oven.

4. Heat 4 tbsp. oil in the frying pan over medium high heat. When the oil is hot, add the beef slivers. Stir quickly and separate the slices while cooking. When the color of the meat changes, stir another ½ minute. Remove and pour on the top of the broccoli. Serve immediately.

牛肉炒雪豆

SNOW PEAS WITH BEEF

¾ lb. tenderloin beef or flank steak

(a) 2½ tbsp. soy sauce
    dash of ginger powder
    dash of garlic powder
  1 tbsp. cornstarch
  1 tbsp. sherry
  1 tsp. sugar
  ½ tsp. sesame oil or vegetable oil

¼ lb. snow peas or 1 package frozen pea pods
3 scallions, cut in 2-inch sections
6 tbsp. vegetable oil, peanut oil, or corn oil

(b) ¼ tsp. salt
  1 tsp. sugar
  2 tbsp. chicken broth or stock
  1 tsp. sherry
  ½ tsp. monosodium glutamate (optional)

1. Trim the fat off of the beef and cut the beef into thin slices. Marinate the beef slices with ingredients (a). Mix well and let stand in the refrigerator at least ½ hour.

2. If you get fresh snow peas, pinch and remove the tips and stems. If you get frozen pea pods, defrost and rinse the pea pods in cold water. Drain well. Heat 2 tbsp. oil in a frying pan over medium high heat. When the oil is hot, add the snow peas, ¼ tsp. salt and 1 tbsp. chicken broth. Stir-fry about ½ minute or until done. Remove peas and set aside.

3. Heat 4 tbsp. oil in a frying pan over medium high heat. When the oil is hot, add the beef. Stir quickly and separate the slices. When the color of the meat changes, add the peas, ingredients (b), and the scallions. Stir quickly and heat thoroughly. Serve hot.

洋葱炒牛肉絲

SWEET ONIONS WITH BEEF SHREDS

½ lb. flank steak

(a) 2 tbsp. soy sauce
     1 tsp. sugar
     ½ tsp. sesame oil
     1 tbsp. cornstarch
     1 tbsp. sherry

1 lb. sweet onions

(b) 1 tsp. salt or to taste
     ½ tsp. monosodium gluta-
        mate (optional)
     1 tbsp. sherry
     ¼ cup chicken broth or stock

(c) 1 tsp. cornstarch
     2 tsp. water

vegetable or corn oil

1. Partially freeze the beef before cutting (if beef is already frozen, thaw until beef is sliceable). Cut the steak across the grain into slices, then cut the slices into shreds, mix the shreds with ingredients (a) well and let stand in the refrigerator at least ½ hour.

2. Peel and cut the onions into halves, then into shreds.

3. Heat 4 tbsp. oil in a frying pan over medium high heat. When the oil is hot, add the meat. Stir about ½ minute, separating the shreds. When the beef almost loses its redness (do not overcook), remove the beef and set aside.

4. Add the remaining 2 tbsp. oil into the frying pan over medium high heat. When the oil is hot, add the onions and fry about 1 minute. Combine ingredients (b) and add to the onions. Stir-fry the mixture until the onions become translucent, but not too soft. Return the beef shreds to the pan and stir thoroughly.

5. Blend ingredients (c) into a paste and add to the pan. Stir until thickened. Serve hot.

蠔油牛肉

BEEF IN OYSTER SAUCE

12 oz. flank steak

(a)　1 tbsp. sherry
　　　3 tbsp. soy sauce
　　　1 tbsp. cornstarch
　　　1 tsp. sugar
　　　½ tsp. sesame oil (or 1 tbsp.
　　　　　vegetable oil)

6 scallions, cut into 2-inch lengths
2 slices ginger

(b)　2 tbsp. oyster sauce
　　　½ tsp. monosodium gluta-
　　　　　mate (optional)
　　　1 tbsp. sherry

(c)　1 tsp. cornstarch
　　　1 tbsp. water

6 tbsp. vegetable, corn or peanut
oil

1. Remove and discard the fat and membrane from the steak. Cut the beef across the grain into bite-sized slices (it is easier to cut if the meat is partially frozen). Marinate the beef with ingredients (a). Mix well and let stand in the refrigerator at least ½ hour.

2. Heat 4 tbsp. oil in a frying pan over medium high heat. When the oil is hot, add the beef mixture, cook, separate the meat slices and stir about 1 minute constantly. When the meat is half cooked, remove and set aside.

3. Add the remaining 1 tbsp. oil to the frying pan over medium high heat. Add the ginger and scallions. Cook about 20 seconds, then add ingredients (b). Stir quickly. Return the beef to the pan and stir thoroughly. Blend ingredients (c) into a paste and add to the pan. Stir-fry until mixture thickens. Serve hot.

BEEF WITH GREEN PEPPER (PEPPER STEAK)

1 lb. flank steak (preferable) or
round steak
2 medium sweet green peppers
3 medium tomatoes

(a) 3 tbsp. soy sauce
     1 tsp. sugar
     ½ tsp. sesame oil
        dash garlic powder
        dash ginger powder
     1 tbsp. sherry (optional)
     1 tbsp. cornstarch

(b) 1 tsp. salt or salt to taste
     ½ tsp. monosodium gluta-
        mate (optional)

4 tbsp. vegetable oil

1. Cut the flank steak against the grain into slices. (If the meat is partially frozen, it will be easier to cut.) Marinate in ingredients (a) very well. Let stand about ½ hour in the refrigerator or a cold place.

2. Scoop away the seeds and white stems from the green peppers. Wash and cut into ½ inch wide strips. Then cut each strip into ½ inch to 1 inch pieces. Put them in boiling water and boil about 1-2 minutes. Drain under cold running water until the peppers are cold. This stops further cooking of the pepper and sets its green color. This can be done ahead of the actual cooking time.

3. Wash the tomatoes and cut into wedges. Then cut each wedge in half, about 1-1½ inch chunks.

4. Heat the 3 tbsp. oil in the frying pan over the medium high heat. When the oil is hot, put the beef into it. Stir quickly and separate into individual pieces. When the meat color changes, remove and set aside.

5. Heat the remaining oil in the pan over medium high heat. When the oil is hot, add the pepper and tomatoes. Then add ingredients (b), stir and heat thoroughly for 1 to 1½ minutes. Then return the beef to the pan. Stir quickly about ½ minute. Serve hot.

牛肉辣汁燒豆腐

BEEF AND BEAN CURD WITH HOT SAUCE

½ lb. ground lean beef
6 squares white bean curd

(a)　½ cup chopped scallions
　　　1 tbsp. chopped fresh ginger
　　　　roots
　　　½ tbsp. chopped garlic (op-
　　　　tional)
　　　2 tbsp hot bean sauce or ½
　　　　tbsp. dry crushed hot pep-
　　　　per
　　　4 dried Chinese mushrooms

4 tbsp. soy sauce
½ cup chicken broth
1 tsp. monosodium glutamate (op-
　　tional)
salt to taste
4 tbsp. vegetable oil

(b)　1 tbsp. cornstarch
　　　1 tbsp. water

1. Rinse and drain the bean curd. Crush the bean curd to a pulp and set aside.

2. Soak the mushrooms in boiling water about 15 to 20 minutes. Drain and squeeze them to extract most of the moisture. Cut off the tough stems. Chop the caps into dices.

3. Heat 4 tbsp. oil in a frying pan over medium high heat. When it is hot, add the beef. Stir quickly to separate the pieces. Then add the soy sauce and stir quickly. Add ingredients (a). Stir and add ½ cup chicken broth. When it boils, add the crushed bean curd and mushrooms. Cook about 1 minute and add the monosodium glutamate. Cook and stir about 2 or 3 minutes.

4. Blend ingredients (b) into a paste and add it to the pan. Stir constantly until thickened. If it is not salty enough, add some salt to taste. Serve hot.

NOTE: Fresh red and green long hot pepper can be chopped and substituted for the hot sauce.

牛肉炒粉絲

BEEF WITH VERMICELLI (BEAN THREAD)

½ lb. flank steak, well trimmed
4 oz. vermicelli (bean thread)

(a)　3 tbsp. soy sauce
　　　1 tsp. sugar
　　　½ tsp. sesame oil (or vegeta-
　　　　　ble oil)
　　　1 tbsp. cornstarch

(b)　¼ cup chicken broth
　　　3 tbsp. wood ears
　　30 stems of tiger lilies
　　　5 scallions, cut into 2-inch
　　　　　sections
　　　1 green pepper
　　　4 slices ginger root (or ¼ tsp.
　　　　　ginger powder)

(c)　1 tbsp. soy sauce
　　　½ tsp. salt (or salt to taste)
　　　½ tsp. monosodium gluta-
　　　　　mate (optional)

¼ tsp. white or black pepper
6 tbsp. vegetable or corn oil

1. Cut the vermicelli (also called cellophane noodles, transparent noodles, or bean threads) into shorter sections with scissors and separate any noodles that cling together. Place the vermicelli into a big bowl and soak in boiling water for several hours. When the vermicelli is soft, drain, cover and set aside.

2. When the frozen beef begins to thaw, cut across the grain into shreds. Combine the beef shreds with ingredients (a). Mix well and let stand at least ½ hour in the refrigerator.

3. Soak the tiger lily stems and wood ears about 15 minutes in boiling water in separate bowls. Cut the tiger lily stems into halves if long.

4. Core and remove the seeds of the green pepper. Cut into shreds. Boil a few minutes and rinse with cold water. Drain and set aside.

5. Heat 4 tbsp. oil in a frying pan over medium high heat. When the oil is hot, add the beef shreds. Stir quickly about ½ minute and separate the shreds until they lose their redness. Remove the meat and leave the oil, if any, in the pan.

6. Add the remaining oil to the pan over medium high heat. When the oil is hot, add the vermicelli. Stir to coat with oil. Add ingredients (b), and stir quickly about ½ minute. Add ingredients (c) and stir thoroughly. Return the beef shreds to the pan and stir well. Sprinkle with black pepper and stir for a few seconds. Place in serving dish and serve hot.

五香牛肉

RED COOKED BEEF

C: 8-10 Servings
W: 4-5 Servings

4 or 5 lbs. shin beef or shank beef
½ cup sherry

(a)   1 cup soy sauce
1 cup chicken broth or water
1½ tbsp. chopped scallions
4 or 5 slices ginger root (if obtainable)
1 star anise

2 tbsp. sugar
salt to taste

1. Scald beef in boiling water for 5 minutes. Take out the beef and pour away the water.

2. Place the beef in a big heavy pot over medium high heat with ingredients (a), turning the meat around in the sauce several times. After the sauce boils, add the ½ cup sherry and turn the heat to very low and simmer about 1 hour. Add the 2 tbsp. sugar and salt. If the sauce is not salty enough, salt to taste. Simmer another 1 to 1½ hour or until done. The meat is done when easily pierced with the tip of a sharp knife. Remember to turn the beef over every half hour while simmering.

3. After the beef is done, slice and serve with its gravy.

NOTE: This beef is equally good when served cold.

草菇和玉米笋炒牛肉

BEEF WITH STRAW MUSHROOMS AND BABY SWEET CORN

1 lb. club steak

(a) 3-4 tbsp. soy sauce
   1 tbsp. sherry
   1 tsp. sugar
   ½ tsp. sesame oil
      dash of ginger powder (op-tional)
      dash of garlic powder (op-tional)
   1 tbsp. cornstarch

1 15 oz. can straw mushrooms
1 15 oz. can baby sweet corn

(b) ¼ cup chicken broth
   ½ tsp. monosodium gluta-mate (optional)
      dash of salt
   1 tsp. sugar

½ tsp. salt
1 tsp. sherry
1 package frozen pea pods (or 4 oz. fresh snow peas)
6 tbsp. vegetable oil

1. Dice the club steak into ½-inch cubes and pound each cube lightly on all sides with the back of a cleaver or kitchen knife. Combine the beef cubes with ingredients (a), toss to coat and set aside in a cold place or the refrigerator at least ½ hour. Turn occasionally.

2. Drain the straw mushrooms and baby sweet corn from cans and set aside.

3. Defrost the pea pods and wash and rinse. Drain well and set aside.

4. Heat 4 tbsp. oil in a frying pan over medium high heat. When the oil is hot, add the beef cubes. Stir-fry about two minutes or a little longer until well done. Remove the meat and leave the oil, if any, in the pan.

5. Add the remaining 2 tbsp. oil in the pan over medium high heat. When the oil is hot, add the pea pods and salt. Stir-fry about ½ minute. Add the straw mushrooms, baby sweet corn and ingredients (b). Stir-fry about 1 minute. Add sherry and return the beef cubes to the pan. Stir thoroughly and cook about 2 minutes. Serve hot.

紅燒牛肉

C: 10-12 Servings
W: 8 Servings

STEWED BEEF CUBES

2-3 lbs. beef cubes, about 1½-2 inch chunks

(a) ¾ cup soy sauce
1½ cups water or stock
half star anise
5 slices ginger root (if obtainable) or ¼ tsp. ginger powder

½ cup sherry

(b) 2 tbsp. sugar
½ tsp. monosodium glutamate (optional)

1. Scald beef cubes in boiling water for 2 minutes. Rinse in cold water and drain well.

2. Place the beef cubes in a big pot. Add mixture (a) and bring to a boil over medium high heat. Add sherry and bring to a boil again. Then turn to low heat, cover and simmer about 1 hour. Add ingredients (b) and cook another ½ hour or until tender. If you like it saltier, add more salt. If you like it sweeter, add more sugar. Serve hot.

NOTE: This dish can be served with plain noodles in a bowl. Pour the beef cubes with sauce on the noodles and add some cooked vegetables such as celery cabbage, Chinese cabbage, or spinach. This is a delicious lunch. If you can not get Chinese noodles, very thin spaghetti is a good substitute.

6

PORK

烤排骨

ROAST SPARERIBS

3-4 lbs. lean spareribs

(a) 4 tbsp. soy sauce
     4 tbsp. hoisin sauce
     2 tbsp. sherry
     ¼ tsp. salt or salt to taste
     4 tbsp. chicken stock or chicken broth
     ¼ tsp. garlic powder, dash of ginger powder
     3 tbsp. honey or 2 tsp. sugar

2 or 3 cups hot water

1. Wash ribs. Trim fat and gristle from ribs and discard. Cut off the soft bones if there are any. To allow better roasting, notch 1 to 2-inch slits on the thicker side of the spareribs.

2. Marinate the spareribs in a long shallow dish with ingredients (a). Rub the sauce evenly on the spareribs. Let stand in the refrigerator for several hours or overnight. During this time, turn the spareribs several times.

3. Preheat the oven to 325°F. Put 2 or 3 cups of hot water into a roast pan on which there is a rack. Place the spareribs on the rack and put the roast pan into the oven for 20 minutes. Turn over and brush the other side with the remaining sauce. Add more hot water to the roast pan, if necessary. Continue to roast another 20 to 30 minutes depending on the thickness of the spareribs. When the ribs are cooked, turn the oven to 400°F and roast the ribs until golden brown (a few minutes).

4. Cut into strips and serve plain or with plum sauce. (See index.)

蕃汁排骨

SPARERIBS WITH TOMATO SAUCE

1½ lbs. spareribs
  6 cups vegetable oil

(a) ½ tbsp. salt or salt to taste
    ½ tsp. monosodium gluta-
       mate (optional)
    ½ tsp. black pepper
    1 tbsp. soy sauce
    1 tbsp. sherry
    ¼ tsp. garlic powder

3 tbsp. cornstarch

(b) 1 tsp. white vinegar
    2 tbsp. ketchup
    3 tsp. sugar
    ½ tsp. sesame oil
    ½ cup chicken broth or stock

(c) 1½ tsp. cornstarch
    2 tsp. water

1. Have the butcher cut the spareribs into two or three equal parts. Then cut into bone strips so each rib is 1½-inches long. Trim the fat and gristle and discard. Marinate the spareribs in ingredients (a) for several hours or overnight in the refrigerator. Toss them once or twice for even marinating. Then coat with the 3 tbsp. cornstarch.

2. Heat oil in a deep frying pan over medium high heat, or deep fryer at 350°F. When the oil is hot (a piece of bread dropped into the oil will form bubbles), place the spareribs in it. Fry about 5 or 6 minutes and remove with slotted spoon. Then refry the spareribs for another minute or until brown and crisp. Remove and drain on paper towels.

3. Heat 1 tbsp. oil in the frying pan over medium heat. Add ingredients (b) and spareribs. Stir thoroughly until mixed. Add ingredients (c) and stir constantly until thickened. Serve hot.

紅燒蹄膀

RED COOKED SHOULDER HAM
(OR PICNIC)

5-6 lb. shoulder ham
¾ cup soy sauce
2 cups boiling water
1 big piece rock candy or 2 tbsp.
   sugar
¼ cup sherry
1 tbsp. vegetable oil
1 star anise (optional)
1½ tsp. salt or salt to taste

1. Heat 2 tbsp. oil in a big frying pan over medium high heat. When the oil is hot, place the shoulder ham on it. When the skin of the meat turns brown, turn the meat over to brown the other side. Fry until all the sides of the ham turn brown.

2. Place the ham into a big pot over medium high heat. Pour soy sauce over the meat until all the sides are coated. Pour the boiling water along the edge of the pot to the bottom. (Do not pour the water over the ham or it will wash away the soy sauce.) Cover to cook. When the sauce boils, add the ¼ cup sherry and the star anise. Turn to low heat and simmer about 15 minutes. Taste the sauce. If it is not salty enough, add 1½ tsp. salt or until it suits your taste. Simmer another 15 minutes and then check the sauce. If the sauce is too low, add some boiling water and simmer again. After 15 minutes add the rock candy or sugar. Simmer again, turning the ham every ½ hour until tender. Make sure the sauce saturates the meat. After 3 hours, turn the heat to very low (*warm* on the electric range) and cook another hour. For the last 15 minutes, simmer the ham uncovered. Slice the ham and serve hot.

NOTE: 1. The dish can be reheated.
   2. If you want to add the Chinese salt vegetables, add to the ham ½ hour after the sugar is added.
   3. If only a 2 lb. shoulder ham is used, reduce the soy sauce to 4 tbsp., water to 1 cup, sherry to 2 tbsp., sugar to 1 tbsp., anise to ½ star and salt to ½ tsp. The method is the same. The cooking time is about 1½-2 hours at very low heat.

甜
酸
肉

Sweet and Sour Pork (p. 56)

中國烹飪

中國烹飪

熊 余 文 琴 著

紅燒排骨

Red-Cooked Spareribs (p. 63)

中國烹飪

中國烹飪

熊 余文琴 著

STEAMED PORK WITH SPICY RICE POWDER

2 lbs. tenderloin or boneless
pork butt
8 tbsp. soy sauce
1 tsp. sugar
4 tbsp. sherry
½ tsp. salt
1½ cups spicy rice powder

1. To prepare the spicy rice powder:

   2 cups medium grain rice
   1 cup glutinous rice
   1 tbsp. star anise

   Wash and rinse both kinds of rice and drain well. Wash the star anise and drain. Roast both kinds of rice and the star anise in a frying pan over medium high heat. Continue stirring and shaking the pan until the mixture becomes crispy and golden brown. Transfer the mixture to an electric blender. Blend the rice mixture at low speed until the mixture is the size of bread crumbs (not fine particles). The rice powder can be stored in a jar for use when needed. (This rice powder can be bought ready made in most Chinese groceries.)

2. Cut the pork into pieces about 2 x 2 x ⅓ inches. Marinate the pork pieces in the soy sauce, sugar, salt and sherry. Let stand in the refrigerator overnight, occasionally stirring.

3. Remove the pork pieces one at a time from the marinade without draining and dip in ¾ of the rice powder, coating each piece thoroughly. Put all the coated pieces compactly in a shallow bowl which will fit inside the top of a steamer (or a shallow pan with a frame on the bottom). Add the remaining rice powder to the bowl, covering the meat. Pour any remaining marinade over the mixture. Sprinkle ½ cup water evenly over the top of the pork mixture. (Soda bottles with sprinkler attachments work well.)

4. Place the bowl in the steamer. Cover and cook over high heat. After the water boils, turn to medium heat. Simmer about 1½-2 hours or until tender. Every half-hour, loosen the meat with a fork or chopstick, in order to let the water vapor reach all the pieces of meat. Test the meat; when the meat is tender, the dish is ready to serve.

NOTE: This dish can be resteamed. You can prepare it the first day and reheat it the next day before serving.

甜酸肉

SWEET AND SOUR PORK

1 lb. boneless pork butt or tenderloin (increase the amount of
pork according to amount of
fat present—1 lb. of actual
pork cubes is necessary)

(a) 2 tsp. sherry
½ tsp. salt
dash of pepper

(b) 1 cup flour
½ cup cornstarch
1 tsp. baking powder
2 tbsp. beaten egg
¾ cup water (if batter is too
thick, add 1-2 tbsp. more)
2 tsp. vegetable oil
½ tsp. salt

1 small onion, sliced and fried for
1 or 2 minutes
1 cup pineapple chunks (canned in
natural juice)
1 cup green peppers
1 cup carrots
1 slice ginger
1 clove garlic, crushed

(c) 2 tbsp. soy sauce
½ cup sugar
1 tsp. salt
3 tbsp. white vinegar
1 tsp. monosodium gluta-
mate (optional)
¼ cup ketchup
¾ cup water
½ cup pineapple juice

(d) 2-3 tbsp. cornstarch
3 tbsp. water
4 cups oil for deep frying

1. Trim the fat and gristle off the pork and discard. Cut into one-inch cubes. Pound each piece of pork lightly with the back of a kitchen knife. Place the meat in a mixing bowl. Mix thoroughly with ingredients (a) and let stand at least ½ hour.

2. Mix ingredients (b) together except water. Slowly add the ¾ cup water to the mixture while blending it by hand. The batter should be smooth, but not watery. Otherwise, the batter will not adhere to the meat.

3. Heat the oil in a shallow pan over a medium heat or in a deep fryer (350°F). Drop a piece of bread into the oil. When bubbles form on the bread, the oil temperature is right for deep frying. Dip each pork cube into the batter. Coat all sides of the pork cube. Clamp the batter-coated meat with chopsticks or ice tongs in the oil for a moment before dropping it into the oil (This will keep the meat from sticking to the bottom and sides of the pot). Cook about 5-8 minutes until the cube floats on the surface and becomes golden brown and crispy. Drain oil from the pork and place on the paper towel. (For the best results, just before serving, heat the oil again on high heat and refry the pork about 1-2 minutes. The pork cubes will be really crispy and delicious.) Keep warm in oven while making sauce.

4. Peel the carrots. Cut into rolling-cut pieces (see chapter 1). Cook in boiling water for 2-3 minutes. Rinse in cold running water. Drain and set aside.

5. Wash and core the green peppers. Discard the seeds. Cut into 1-inch pieces. Soak in boiling water about 1-2 minutes. Drain and rinse in cold running water to chill.

6. Combine the pineapple chunks (save the juice for the sweet and sour sauce), carrots, onions and green peppers. Set aside.

7. Heat 2 tbsp. oil in a frying pan. Brown the ginger and garlic for a minute. Discard. Add ingredients (c) and stir thoroughly. Add the pineapple chunks, carrots, onions and green peppers. Blend the mixture (d) into a paste and add to the sauce. Stir constantly until the sauce is thickened.

8. Pour sauce over meat cubes. Serve immediately!

NOTE: The fried pork cubes can be frozen. Before serving, thaw 5-8 minutes and immediately refry 4-5 minutes or until golden brown and crispy. The pork cubes will be crisp and tasty.

木犀肉

MOO-SHI MEAT

½ lb. shredded pork
30 pieces tiger lily stems
4 tbsp. wood ears
6 dried black mushrooms
½ cup shredded bamboo shoots
4 scallions, cut into 2-inch sections
1 cup shredded Chinese cabbage (optional)

(a)   3 tbsp. soy sauce
     1 tbsp. sherry
     1 tsp. cornstarch

(b) ½ tsp. salt
     ½ tsp. sugar

(c) ½ tsp. monosodium glutamate (optional)
     1 tsp. salt (or salt to taste)

3 slices ginger root (if obtainable) or ¼ tsp. ginger powder
4 eggs
5 tbsp. vegetable or corn oil
Chinese pancakes (see index)

1. Marinate the meat slices with ingredients (a) very well, and let stand in the refrigerator for ½ hour.

2. Soak the wood ears, tiger lily stems and black mushrooms in boiling water in separate bowls for about 15-20 minutes. Cut off the hard tips from the mushrooms and the hard parts of the tiger lily stems and discard. Cut the mushroom caps into slices, tiger lily stems into halves, and break the wood ears into small pieces.

3. Beat the egg well with ingredients (b) and set aside.

4. Heat 2 tbsp. oil in the frying pan over medium heat. When the oil is hot, add the ginger slices and stir. Add the beaten eggs and stir quickly into the scrambled stage with a flat spatula. Remove from the pan.

5. Heat the remaining oil in the frying pan over medium high heat. When the oil is hot, add the meat shreds. Stir quickly and separate the shreds. When the meat color changes, add the scallions, Chinese cabbage, bamboo shoots, wood ears, tiger lily stems and mushrooms. Stir-fry for a moment and add ingredients (c). Stir thoroughly. If it is not salty enough, salt to taste. Stir and cook a couple of minutes. Add the scrambled eggs to the pan and stir well, about ½ minute. Serve with Chinese pancakes.

紅燒肉

C: 6-8 Servings
W: 4 Servings

RED-COOKED PORK

2 lbs. boneless pork butt or ten-derloin
1 cup cold water
¼ cup sherry
½ cup soy sauce
2 tbsp. sugar
4 slices ginger
½ star anise
¾ tsp. salt or salt to taste

1. Cut the meat into about 1½-inch chunks. Scald the meat in boiling water for about 2 minutes. Then rinse with cold water and drain.

2. Put the meat in a pot and add the water and soy sauce. Bring to a boil. Add the sherry, the ginger and the star anise, and turn to low heat. Cover and simmer about 30 minutes. Taste the sauce. If it is not salty enough, add salt to taste. Add sugar and cover. Cook on low heat (or warm if using an electric range), about 40 minutes or until the meat is tender. Serve hot.

NOTE: 1. Red-cooked pork can be stored in the refrigerator a few days and reheated when needed.
2. If you like the sauce thicker, cook the meat partially uncovered until the sauce is reduced to ¾ cup.
3. For darker colored meat, add dark soy sauce.
4. Variations with Red-cooked pork:
   a) Meat sauce with boiled noodles—add 2 cups water instead of 1 cup water.
   b) Add carrots, turnip chunks or white radishes to the red-cooked pork mixture 20 minutes before the meat is done (20 minutes after the sugar is added).

魚香肉絲

SHREDDED PORK WITH HOT SAUCE

12 oz. boneless pork butt, tenderloin, or loin (increase the
amount of pork according
to the amount of fat
present—12 oz. of actual
pork shreds is necessary)

(a)   2 tbsp. soy sauce
     1 tsp. sherry
     1 tbsp. cornstarch

    ¼ cup wood ears
15-20 water chestnuts (canned)
     1 tbsp. chopped scallion
     1 tbsp. chopped ginger or ¼
     tsp. ginger powder
     2 cloves crushed garlic or ¼
     tsp. garlic powder
     5 tbsp. vegetable or corn oil

(b)   1 tbsp. sherry
     2 tbsp. soy sauce
   ¼-½ tbsp. salt (or salt to taste)
     1 tsp. cornstarch
     1 tsp. sesame oil
     1 tbsp. sugar
    ¼ tsp. monosodium gluta-
     mate (optional)
     1 tbsp. hot soybean paste

1. Partially freeze the pork. Cut across the grain into slices. Then cut the slices into shreds the size of matchsticks. Place in bowl and marinate with ingredients (a). Let the mixture stand in the refrigerator at least 30 minutes.

2. Soak the wood ears in boiling water about 15 minutes. Drain and cut into shreds. Cut the water chestnuts into shreds.

3. Heat 3 tbsp. oil in a frying pan over medium high heat. When the oil is hot, add the pork shreds and stir quickly, separating the shreds. When the meat color changes (about ½-1 minute), remove and set aside.

4. Heat the remaining 2 tbsp. oil in the frying pan over medium high heat. Add ginger and garlic and stir. Add the meat shreds, wood ears, water chestnuts, and ingredients (b). Stir thoroughly. Salt to taste. Add the chopped scallions and stir evenly and constantly. Serve hot.

NOTE: For people who like very spicy dishes, add 1-2 more tbsp. of hot soybean paste.

甜火腿

C: 10-12 Servings
W: 5-6 Servings

SWEET HAM

2 lb. Smithfield ham
4 tbsp. rock candy, crushed
1 8-oz. can pineapple rings
½ tsp. soy sauce
1 tbsp. cornstarch
3 tbsp. water
1 tbsp. vegetable oil

1. Place the ham in a pot and cover with water. Cook on medium high heat. When the water boils, turn to very low heat. Cover and simmer about 1 to 1½ hours. Then drain.

2. Cut the ham into ½-inch thick slices. Discard the bone or save it for cooking soup.

3. Arrange the ham slices in a round or square heatproof container. Sprinkle with crushed rock candy and the pineapple juice from the can of pineapple. Place the container in the top of a steamer and cover with the steamer lid. Cook over medium high heat. When the water boils, turn to medium heat. Steam about 20 to 30 minutes until the sugar is melted.

4. Remove the ham slices to a platter. (Save the accumulated liquid in the dish.) Garnish the ham with the pineapple rings.

5. Transfer the liquid from the container to a pan over medium high heat. Blend the cornstarch with water and add to the liquid. Add the soy sauce and stir until thickened. Add the oil and stir. Immediately pour over the ham. Serve hot.

獅子頭

LION HEADS (PORK MEATBALLS)

2 lbs. ground pork

(a)   ⅓ **cup soy sauce**
     3 **tbsp. water**
     4 **stalks scallion, chopped fine**
     1 **tsp. fresh ginger (chopped fine) or ½ tsp. ginger powder**
     2 **tbsp. sherry**
     ½ **tsp. monosodium glutamate (optional)**
     1 **large egg**
     2 **tbsp. cornstarch**
   15-20 **water chestnuts, minced**

6 tbsp. vegetable oil
2 lbs. celery cabbage
1 tsp. salt or salt to taste

(b)   4 **tbsp. cornstarch**
     3 **tbsp. water**

(c)   1 **cup water**
     1 **tbsp. soy sauce**
     1 **tsp. sugar**

1. Buy the boneless Boston butt or pork butt. Ask the butcher to grind it once (only once) for you. If you grind it yourself, be sure to trim off the gristle before grinding.

2. Mix the ground pork with ingredients (a). Use fingers to mix very well. Let stand at least ½ hour.

3. Divide the meat mixture into 8 portions. Form each portion of the meat mixture into large balls. Roll each meat ball in the paste of ingredients (b).

4. Pour 4 tbsp. oil into a frying pan over medium heat. Brown the meatballs in the frying pan. Always loosen the bottom first with the back of spatula and turn carefully.

5. Remove the meatballs gently to a deep pot. Save the sauce in the frying pan. Put ingredients (c) into the pot. When the liquid boils, cover and simmer over low heat about 1½ hour or until the meatballs are done.

6. Wash the cabbage and cut into 2-inch sections. Heat the sauce left in the frying pan over medium high heat. Put the cabbage into the pan and cook for several minutes. Arrange the cabbage in another big pot along with the sauce. Set the cooked meatballs on top of the cabbage. Pour the liquid from the meatballs over the cabbage. Cover and cook on medium high heat. When the liquid boils, turn to low heat and simmer about 8-10 minutes. Serve hot.

NOTE: For Lion Heads, the proportion of the fat and lean meat in ground pork is ¾ of lean and ¼ of fat.

紅燒排骨

C: 8-10 Servings
W: 4-6 Servings

RED-COOKED SPARERIBS

2½ lbs. spareribs

(a) **4 tbsp. soy sauce**
½-¾ cup water
½ tsp. salt or salt to taste
2 tbsp. sherry
1 slice ginger

½ star anise (if obtainable)
1 tbsp. sugar

1. Ask the butcher to cut the bones into three equal parts. Then cut into strips, so each rib is 1½-inches long. Trim the fat and gristle and discard.

2. Put the ribs, ingredients (a) and the star anise into a big pot over medium high heat. Bring to a boil. Then turn to low heat, cover, and simmer 30 minutes. Add the sugar and stir thoroughly. Partially cover and simmer about 20-30 minutes or until done. If there is still a lot of juice left, turn to medium high heat and stir constantly until most of the liquid has evaporated and all the juice seems to have wrapped around the meat.

3. Place the spareribs on a platter and serve hot.

家常豆腐

PORK AND BEAN CURD, HOME STYLE

6 oz. lean pork
6 squares of bean curd

(a) 2 tbsp. soy sauce
　　 dash of ginger powder
　　 dash of garlic powder
　 ½ tsp. sugar
　 ¼ tsp. sesame oil

(b) 2 tbsp. wood ears
　 ½ oz. dry shrimp (if obtaina-
　　 ble)
　 2 scallions
　 5 hot peppers (or more if
　　 desired)
　 ¼ cup bamboo shoots, cut
　　 into slices

(c) 1 tsp. sugar
　 2 tbsp. soy sauce
　 ½ tsp. monosodium gluta-
　　 mate (optional)
　 1 tsp. sherry
　 6 tbsp. chicken broth
　 1 tsp. salt or salt to taste

(d) 1 tsp. cornstarch
　 1 tsp. water

8 tbsp. vegetable oil

1. Wash the bean curd squares. Dry them with paper towels. (Dry each of them very well.) Cut each bean curd into 4 equal squares. Further cut each of the 4 squares from the side, reducing the thickness and producing two equally thick squares. (That means that each bean curd is cut into 8 equal squares, so that altogether there will be 48 small bean curd squares.)

2. The pork is easier to cut if partially frozen. Cut the meat against the grain into 1 x 1 x 1/10-inch slices. Marinate in ingredients (a). Toss well and let stand in the refrigerator at least ½ hour.

3. Soak the dry shrimp in warm water about 15 minutes. Soak the wood ears in boiling water about ½ hour. Wash the red peppers and remove the cores

and take away their seeds. Then cut each red pepper into about 2-inch sections.

4. Pour 5 tbsp. oil into a frying pan over medium high heat. When the oil is hot, carefully put the bean curd into the pan over low heat. Cook until their color turns golden brown. Turn the squares to cook the other sides until golden brown. Remove the bean curds and leave the oil in the pan.

5. Place the frying pan with the remaining oil over medium high heat. Add 1 tbsp. oil. When the oil is very hot, add the meat, stir quickly and separate each piece. After the meat changes color, remove and set aside.

6. Put 2 tbsp. oil into the pan over medium high heat. When the oil is hot, add ingredients (b). Stir quickly for a while. Return the bean curd and add ingredients (c). Stir thoroughly. Taste the bean curd to check if it is salty enough. If not, salt to taste. Return the meat. Add the paste ingredients (d). Stir quickly until thickened. Serve hot.

NOTE: If the dish looks too dry, add 1 tbsp. vegetable oil before putting on the serving plate.

义烧肉〈一〉

C: 6-8 Servings
W: 3-4 Servings

ROAST PORK I

2 lbs. lean pork butt or tenderloin
2 tbsp. hoisin sauce
3 tbsp. soy sauce

1. Trim the fat and gristle from the meat. Cut the meat against the grain into ½ inch thick pieces. Due to the irregular size of the pork, the size of the ½ inch thick pieces may vary. Rub the meat with 2 tbsp. hoisin sauce and 3 tbsp. soy sauce. Marinate the meat for several hours. Turn the meat over from time to time.

2. Put the meat and sauce into a 9"x11" baking pan. Cover with aluminum foil.

3. Preheat the oven to 350°F. Put the pan on the middle shelf of the oven. Roast about 1¼ hours. Turn the meat over every ½ hour. After about 1¼ hours, turn the oven to 300°F, uncover and roast about 10 to 15 minutes. Cut into small pieces. Serve hot or cold.

义燒肉〈二〉

ROAST PORK II

**4-5 lbs. boneless lean pork butt,
tenderloin or fillet of pork**

(a) 4 tbsp. hoisin sauce
6 tbsp. soy sauce
¼ tsp. salt
1 tbsp. sherry
1 tbsp. chicken broth
½ tsp. monosodium gluta-
mate (optional)

1. Trim the fat and gristle from the meat. Cut the meat into approximately 5"
x 2" x 1½" strips. Due to the irregular size of the pork, the size of the meat
strips may vary. Rub the meat with the mixture of ingredients (a), and
marinate the meat several hours or overnight. Turn the meat from time to
time.

2. When ready to cook, place the meat pieces on a metal rack over a roasting
pan filled with 2 or 3 cups of hot water. Insert the roast pan into a
preheated over of 300°F for 1-1½ hour or until done. Do not let meat touch
the water. After ½ hour, watch the water in the pan. If it is not enough, add
more hot water.

3. During the cooking time brush the meat with the sauce mixture several
times and turn the meat over several times for even cooking. When the
meat is done (take a fork to test whether the meat is tender), cut against the
grain into slices and serve hot or cold.

NOTE: 1. You can freeze the roast pork for later use. Defrost it when
needed. Wrap the pork in aluminum foil and heat it in a warm
oven.
2. Leftover roast pork can be wrapped tightly and stored in the
freezer for use in steamed buns or fried rice.

辣椒肉絲

PORK WITH HOT PEPPERS

14 oz. pork tenderloin or lean pork
½ lb. hot fresh peppers
6 scallions, cut into 2-inch sections

(a) **3½ tbsp. soy sauce**
    1 tbsp. sherry
    ⅛ tsp. ginger powder
    ⅛ tsp. garlic powder
    1 tsp. sugar
    1 tsp. sesame oil
    1 tbsp. cornstarch

5 tbsp. vegetable or corn oil
¼ tsp. salt or salt to taste

1. Partially freeze the pork tenderloin. Cut across the grain into thin slices, then cut the slices into shreds. Combine the shreds with ingredients (a). Mix well. Let stand in the refrigerator at least ½ hour.

2. Wash and drain the peppers. Trim off the hard top and remove the seeds of the peppers. Cut into thin shreds.

3. Heat the frying pan over medium high heat. Pour in 2 tbsp. oil. When the oil is hot, add the hot pepper shreds and stir-fry about 1 minute. Add the scallions and salt. Stir-fry about 1 minute. If it is not salty enough, add salt to taste. Remove from the pan and set aside.

4. With the same pan, add the remaining 3 tbsp. oil. When it is hot, add the meat shreds. Stir-fry quickly and separate the shreds. When the color of the meat changes, return the hot pepper shreds. Stir and cook about 1-2 minutes. Serve hot.

珍珠丸子

GLUTINOUS RICE BALLS

12 oz. ground pork
1 cup glutinous rice

(a) 2 tbsp. soy sauce
  1 tsp. sesame oil
  2 tsp. sugar
  1 egg white, beaten
  ½ tsp. salt or salt to taste

(b) 8 canned or fresh water
    chestnuts, chopped
  ½ oz. dried shrimp, chopped
    (if obtainable)
  3 tbsp. chopped scallions
  ½ tsp. minced ginger root, or
    ¼ tsp. ginger powder
  1 tsp. cornstarch

2 tbsp. shredded carrots
1 tbsp. chopped parsley

1. Soak the glutinous rice for at least 4 hours. Wash and drain well. Spread
   on a cloth towel and dry.

2. With fingers, mix the ground pork with ingredients (a) in a large bowl for
   5-6 minutes. Then add ingredients (b) and mix very well.

3. Take 1 tbsp. meat and form into a ball shape. Moistening your hands from
   time to time with a little cold water, repeat the process until all the meat
   has been converted to balls. There will be about 32-34 balls.

4. Put the glutinous rice on a flat plate. Roll each meat ball in the glutinous
   rice, pressing down gently but firmly as you roll so that the rice grains
   adhere to the meat. Place them side by side on a strip of wax paper.

5. Put the glutinous rice balls on a plate. Place them in a regular steamer to
   steam about 40 minutes to 1 hour on medium heat. (Calculate the time
   starting from when the water is boiling in the steamer.) Remove balls to a
   warm serving plate. Garnish with shredded carrots and parsley. Serve hot.

NOTE: 1. If you don't have a regular steamer, you can arrange the meat balls on a heatproof plate and place the plate on a rack in a pot. Add water to the bottom of the pot (under the plate) and boil on high heat, covering the pot tightly. Turn to medium heat and steam the meat balls for 40-60 minutes. Set the steaming plate on a larger platter and serve at once.

2. This dish can be cooked in advance and stored in the refrigerator. Before dinner, resteam about 10 to 20 minutes over medium heat (after the water boils).

紅燒豬蹄

C: 6-8 Servings
W: 2-3 Servings

RED COOKED OR STEWED PIG HOCKS

4 lbs. pig hocks

(a) 4 quarts cold water
4 tsp. salt or salt to taste
1½ cups brown sugar
10 slices of fresh ginger
1 tbsp. soy sauce
¼ cup white vinegar

1. Ask the butcher to split the pig hocks in half and cut each half into about 1½- to 2-inch length sections.

2. Place the hocks in a pot and add cold water to cover. Bring to a boil and simmer one minute. Then drain immediately and run under cold water. Drain again. (See Note.)

3. Return the hocks to the pot and add ingredients (a) over medium high heat. When the liquid boils, turn to low heat. Cover and cook about 50 minutes.

4. Uncover and cook at low heat about 1½ to 2 hours or until done. Serve hot.

NOTE: 1. An alternative method to Step 2: When the water boils, use a spoon to skim the impurities and discard. Go to Step 3.

2. This dish can be refrigerated and reheated.

豬肉釀黃瓜

STUFFED CUCUMBERS

3 large cucumbers or 5 medium
ones

(a)   1 lb. ground pork
      ½ tsp. minced fresh ginger
          root or ¼ tsp. ginger pow-
          der
      2 tsp. minced scallions
      2 tbsp. sherry
      2 tbsp. soy sauce
   1½ tsp. sugar
      1 tsp. salt or salt to taste
      1 tsp. monosodium gluta-
          mate (optional)
     4 tbsp. corn flake crumbs
      1 tbsp. cornstarch

(b)   2 tsp. soy sauce
      1 cup chicken broth or stock
      3 tbsp. sherry

(c)   1 tbsp. cornstarch
      2 tbsp. water

flour
3 tbsp. vegetable oil

1. Peel cucumbers, trimming and discarding the ends. Cut into 2-inch
sections. Scoop out seeds from each section and discard.

2. Mix the ground pork well with ingredients (a) for a stuffing.

3. Put the stuffing in the center of each section. Pack it tightly and round out
the edges to prevent the stuffing from slipping out of the cucumber. Dip
the ends in flour.

4. In a frying pan heat 2 tbsp. oil over medium heat. When the oil is hot, put
the ends of the cucumber sections into the pan, and brown both ends of
each section very well.

5. Lay the side of each section in a frying pan. Add ingredients (b). Bring to
boil first over medium high heat. Then turn to low heat and simmer until
tender (about 15 to 20 minutes). Turn once or twice for even cooking.

6. Arrange the cucumber sections on a plate and leave the sauce in the pan. Add the paste of ingredients (c) and stir constantly until thickened. Pour over the cucumbers and serve.

NOTE: This dish can be put in the oven to warm.

鹹蛋蒸肉

C: 3-4 Servings
W: 2-3 Servings

PORK WITH SALTED EGGS

8 oz. ground pork

(a)   1 egg, lightly beaten
¼ cup water
1 tbsp. soy sauce
¼ tsp. salt
2 tsp. cornstarch
2 tsp. sherry

2 salted eggs
1½ tbsp. chopped scallions
2 tbsp. water

1. Place the ground pork in a deep plate, which will fit inside a steamer. Combine the pork with ingredients (a) and mix well with your fingers. Spread the meat around the sides of the plate forming a wall around a center cavity which will contain the yolks of the salted eggs.

2. Break the two eggs, separating the yolks from the egg whites. Place the yolks in the center cavity of the pork and cover the entire mixture with the egg whites. Sprinkle scallions on top.

3. Boil water in the bottom of the steamer over medium high heat. Set the deep dish containing the pork and eggs in the top of the steamer and cover. When the water boils, turn to low heat and cook about 15 minutes. Pour 2 tbsp. of water on top of the egg whites and cover. Cook another 15 minutes over medium heat. Serve immediately.

71

葱爆肉片

SAUTEED PORK WITH SCALLIONS

1 lb. pork tenderloin or country
spareribs

(a) 2 tbsp. soy sauce
½ tbsp. sugar
1 tsp. sherry
1 tbsp. cornstarch

3-4 tbsp. vegetable or corn oil
4-5 scallions

(b) 1 tbsp. soy sauce
1½ tsp. sugar
½ tsp. monosodium gluta-
mate (optional)
dash of pepper
1 tsp. sesame oil
¼ tsp. garlic powder
¼ tsp. ginger powder

1. Remove the fat and gristle from the meat. Cut the lean meat into thin long
   slices (It will be easier to cut if the meat is partially frozen). Using the back
   of the kitchen knife, pound the meat. Marinate the slices with ingredients
   (a). Mix well and let stand in the refrigerator for at least ½ hour.

2. Heat the oil in a frying pan over medium high heat. When it is hot, add the
   pork slices. Stir and separate the slices until the meat loses its red color
   (about ½ minute). If there is not enough oil, add a little bit more.

3. When the meat becomes light brown, add the scallions. Then stir and add
   ingredients (b). Stir a few more seconds and serve.

NOTE: The bones can be used for sparerib soup.

豬肉絲炒豆芽及韭菜

PORK STRIPS WITH LEEKS
AND BEAN SPROUTS

½ lb. lean pork
1 lb. leeks
1 lb. bean sprouts, washed and cleaned (canned may be substituted for fresh.)

(a) 2 tbsp. soy sauce
     1 tbsp. sherry
        dash ginger powder
     ½ tsp. sugar
     ¼ tsp. sesame oil
     1 tsp. cornstarch

(b) 1 tsp. salt or salt to taste
     2 tbsp. soy sauce
     ¼ tsp. monosodium glutamate (optional)

5 tbsp. vegetable oil

1. Cut the pork against the grain into slices, and cut each slice into strips. Mix the pork strips with ingredients (a) very well. Let stand in the refrigerator at least ½ hour.

2. Heat 3 tbsp. vegetable oil in a frying pan over medium high heat. When the oil is hot, add the meat. Stir and separate the individual strips. After the meat changes its color, remove and set aside.

3. Pour the remaining 2 tbsp. oil into the pan over medium high heat. After the oil is hot, add the leeks and bean sprouts and stir quickly for a few seconds. Add ingredients (b) and stir a couple of seconds. Return the meat to the pan and stir thoroughly. Serve hot.

豬肉炒草菇和玉米筍

PORK WITH STRAW MUSHROOMS AND
BABY CORN

1½ lbs. country spareribs

(a)   3 tbsp. soy sauce
     1 tbsp. sherry
     1 tsp. sugar
     ½ tsp. sesame oil
     1 tbsp. cornstarch

1 can straw mushrooms
1 can baby corn
1 tsp. monosodium glutamate
dash of salt to taste
1 tsp. sugar
5 tbsp. vegetable or corn oil

1. Trim off the fat and gristle from the meat and discard. Cut the lean meat across the grain into 1½-inch slices. Marinate the meat slices with ingredients (a). Mix well and let stand at least ½ hour in the refrigerator.

2. Drain the mushrooms and corn. Put in bowl and set aside.

3. Heat 3 tbsp. oil in a frying pan over medium high heat. When the oil is hot, add the meat slices. Stir quickly and separate the slices. When the meat color changes (about 1-2 minutes), remove from pan and set aside.

4. Heat the remaining 2 tbsp. oil in the frying pan over medium high heat. When the oil is hot, add the mushrooms and corn. Stir about ½ minute. Add the sugar and monosodium glutamate. If it is not salty enough, salt to taste. Return the meat to the pan and stir thoroughly, about ½-1 minute longer. Transfer to serving plate and serve.

NOTE: The bones can be used for sparerib soup.

洋葱炒肉絲

PORK SHREDS WITH ONIONS

¼ lb. lean pork tenderloin

(a) 2 tbsp. soy sauce
    dash of ginger powder
    dash of garlic powder
  ½ tsp. sugar
  ¼ tsp. sesame oil
  1 tsp. cornstarch

4 medium sized onions
½ tsp. salt or salt to taste
¼ tsp. monosodium glutamate
(optional)
5 tbsp. vegetable oil or corn oil

1. Partially freeze the pork tenderloin for several hours. (It is easier to cut if the meat is partially frozen.) Cut the meat against the grain into slices. Then cut the slices into shreds. Marinate with ingredients (a). Mix well and let stand in the refrigerator for at least ½ hour.

2. Take off the outer skin of the onions and discard. Cut each onion perpendicularly into halves and then slice. Separate each slice into semicircular strips by hand.

3. Pour 3 tbsp. oil into the frying pan over medium high heat. Sprinkle the ½ tsp. salt into the pan. When the oil is hot, add the onion strips and stir quickly about 1 or 2 minutes until tender (taste one strip). Remove and set aside.

4. Using the same pan, pour in the remaining oil over medium high heat. When the oil is hot, add the meat. Stir quickly and separate the shreds. When the color of the meat changes, add the cooked onions and stir about ½ minute. Turn off the heat. Then remove to serving plate. Serve hot.

麻婆豆腐
GROUND PORK WITH BEAN CURD

8 cubes bean curd
½ lb. ground pork

(a) 2 cloves garlic, finely minced
     or ¼ tsp. garlic powder
     2 tbsp. hot bean paste
     2 tbsp. soy sauce
     1 tsp. salt or to taste
     ⅔ cup chicken broth or stock
     ¼ tsp. monosodium gluta-
     mate (optional)

(b) 2 tsp. cornstarch
     2 tsp. cold water

1 tsp. sesame oil
2 tbsp. scallions, chopped
1 tsp. brown peppercorn powder
   (see note)
5 tbsp. vegetable or corn oil

1. Cut the bean curd into ½-inch cubes and soak in boiling water for 3 minutes. Drain well.

2. Heat 3 tbsp. oil in a frying pan over medium high heat. When the oil is hot, add the ground pork and stir-fry for a few seconds. Add ingredients (a) and the bean curd. Cook for 2-3 minutes.

3. Blend the mixture (b) into paste and add to the pan. Stir constantly until thickened. Then sprinkle with scallions and sesame oil. Stir and place in a warm bowl. Garnish with brown peppercorn powder and serve.

NOTE: You can make brown peppercorn powder as follows.

Place the peppercorns (buy them from Chinese grocery) in a frying pan and cook over medium heat, stirring and shaking the pan until the peppercorns are roasted. Then put them into an electric blender and blend until finely ground. Store the powder in a tightly covered container.

7

POULTRY

南京板鴨

C: 10-12 Servings
W: 10-12 Servings

SALTY NANKING DUCK

1 4-5 lb. duck
4 tbsp. salt
1½ tsp. brown peppercorn
½ tsp. saltpetre (from drug store)

1. Ask the butcher to cut the duck in half. Wash and clean the duck thoroughly. Remove the oil sacs and discard. Wipe dry with paper towels.

2. Mix the salt and peppercorn in a frying pan over medium heat. Stir constantly until the salt becomes light brown and there is an aroma of peppercorn (about 5-10 minutes). Remove from heat and let cool.

3. Mix the mixture of salt and peppercorn with saltpetre very well. Rub the mixture evenly on both sides of the duck. Put the duck, back down, in the refrigerator or a cold place for 4 or 5 days.

4. Hang the two pieces of duck with a string through the tail ends in a cold and windy place, such as a garage or the attic (with ventilation) for about 3 or 4 weeks. (The duck should be very dried out during this time.)

5. When you are ready to prepare the duck, put it in the steamer (see chapter 1) over high heat. When the water boils, turn to medium heat. Steam about 30-40 minutes or until done. Turn over once. Use a fork to test it. (If it is tender, it is done.) Let it cool or put it in refrigerator about 1 hour. Cut (see Instruction 5 on Meats, chapter 2) into 1-1½ inch pieces and serve.

NOTE: 1. The duck can be preserved in the refrigerator for as long as you like.
   2. The best time to do this recipe is in the winter because you can hang it outside for 3 or 4 weeks.
   3. The salty duck can not be used as main dish.

北京烤鴨
PEKING DUCK

1 4-5 lb. duck
¾ cup sherry
1½ tsp. salt

(a) 1 quart water
     ½ cup honey
     6 slices fresh ginger
     3 scallions, cut into 2-inch
       sections

     15 scallions

Duck sauce:

     ¼ cup hoisin sauce
     1 tbsp. chicken broth
     1 tsp. sesame oil
     ½ tsp. monosodium gluta-
       mate (optional)
     1 tsp. sugar

Chinese pancakes: about a dozen (see index)

1. Rinse the duck thoroughly inside and out under cold running water. Pat dry
   with paper towels. Pull out excess fat from the cavity of the duck and
   discard. Cut off the wing tips. Rub inside and outside the duck with 1½
   tsp. salt. Let stand in the refrigerator about 1 hour. Take the duck out and
   wipe the outside skin with paper towels once more. With a heavy hook
   through the tail of the duck (you can use a string instead of a wire) hang it
   in the air about two hours.

2. Heat ingredients (a) in a big pot. When it boils, add the ¾ cup sherry.
   Then holding the duck with the wire, lower it into the boiling liquid. Turn
   the duck side to side until the skin is completely moistened with the liquid,
   about 2 or 3 minutes. Hang the duck in an air space or the basement for 24
   hours or at least overnight; place a pan under the duck to catch the
   drippings. An electric fan can be used to speed the drying time.

3. Set the duck, breast up, on the rack of a roast pan with water in the pan.
   Preheat the oven to 350°F. Put the duck on the rack in the middle of the
   oven. Roast about ¾-1 hour. Replenish the water as needed. When the
   skin becomes light brown, cover the top of the duck with aluminum foil
   and continue roasting for ¾-1 hour. Then turn the oven to 300°F, and turn

the back of the duck up. Roast about 30 minutes until its skin becomes dark brown. Then turn the duck breast up again for 10 or more minutes at 350°F (use a fork or knife to check if the meat is tender). Now remove the fat and water from the bottom of the pan. Roast the breast and the back of the duck at 375°F about 5-10 minutes until crisp.

4. While the duck is roasting in the oven, you can prepare the scallions, the duck sauce, and pancakes (the pancakes can be made ahead and stored in the refrigerator).

(i) Scallions. Trim the roots and then cut the white part of the scallions in 3-inch long sections. Split both ends of the sections with several ½-inch deep cuts, which will open as brushlike fans when stored in ice water in the refrigerator for a few hours. Drain when ready to serve.

(ii) Duck sauce. Mix hoisin sauce, chicken broth, sesame oil, sugar and monosodium glutamate very well. Serve with the duck, steamed pancakes and scallions.

(iii) Take the Chinese pancakes from the refrigerator and steam for 10 minutes over medium high heat before serving.

5. When the duck is ready, with a small knife and your fingers remove the crisp skin from the breast, sides and back of the duck. Cut the skin into 2- by 3-inch rectangular shapes. Arrange them into a single layer on a heated plate. Cut the wings and drumsticks from the duck and cut all the meat away from breast and carcass. Slice the meat into thin pieces and place them with the wings and drumsticks on another heated platter. Serve immediately.

NOTE: The hardest part is the oven problem. Because oven temperatures are variable from one make of stove to another, a close watch must be made of the duck during the entire roasting time.

香酥鴨

CRISPY DUCK

1 4-5 lb. duck

(a) 1 tbsp. salt
     1 tbsp. peppercorns

(b) 5 slices ginger root
     4 scallions, cut into 2-inch
        sections
     1 tbsp. sherry

(c) 3 tbsp. soy sauce
     1 star anise, crushed very
        fine

4-5 cups vegetable oil or corn oil

1. Wash and clean the duck inside and outside. Pull excess fat from the cavity of the duck and discard. Wipe the duck dry with paper towels. Slam the duck down hard on the breast bone to break it and flatten it.

2. Fry ingredients (a) at low heat for 2 or 3 minutes and set aside.

3. Mix ingredients (a) and (b) in a bowl. Rub the duck inside and outside evenly. Let stand for 10 hours or overnight in the refrigerator.

4. After removing the duck from the refrigerator, rub with ingredients (c) very well. Steam the duck in a steamer (see chapter 1) over medium high heat. After the water boils, turn to medium heat. Cover and steam about 1½- 2 hours or until tender. Watch the water in the steamer. If too much boils away, use boiling water to replenish it. Use the tip of a sharp knife to pierce the duck to test whether or not it is tender. If it is tender, remove the duck from the steamer and let it cool for a while. Discard the ginger and scallions. Drain the duck if there is any juice. Dry with paper towels. Let it stand for several hours to dry further.

5. Heat 4-5 cups of vegetable oil in a large deep pot over medium high heat. When the oil is piping hot, place the duck carefully (breast up) in the pot for 5-8 minutes. Turn the duck over (breast down) for another 5-8 minutes or until the duck is golden brown.

6. Remove the duck from the oil and let it cool. Cut it into bite-sized pieces with a cleaver (see Instruction 5 on Meats, chapter 2). Serve with flavored peppercorn salt (see note) and steamed-flavored rolls.

NOTE: Flavored peppercorn salt:
4 tbsp. peppercorns
18 tbsp. salt

Fry the peppercorns and salt over low heat in a dry frying pan until dark brown and aromatic. Blend in an electric blender with low speed into fine powder. You can blend this powder ahead of time and store in an air-tight jar for months.

C: 6-8 Servings
W: 3-4 Servings

烤鴨

ROAST DUCK

1 4-5 lb. duck
3 scallions
⅓ cup soy sauce
1 cup water
3-4 tbsp. sugar

1. Wash and clean the duck inside and outside. Remove the oil sacs and discard. Reserve the giblets for another use.

2. Place the duck in a roast pan, breast side up and back down. Insert the 3 scallions into the stomach of the duck. Pour ⅓ cup soy sauce over the duck. Pour 1 cup of water from the edge of the roast pan. (Do not pour over the duck; otherwise you will wash the soy sauce away. Water is important; otherwise the duck will be too dry.) Sprinkle the duck with 3-4 tbsp. sugar.

3. Preheat the oven at 350°F. Put the duck on the middle shelf of the oven and bake about 2 hours. Every ½ hour, baste the duck with the juice in the roast pan.

4. At the end of the second hour, the duck will be dark brown. Turn oven to 325°F and bake another half hour. The duck is done when its meat is tender to the fork.

5. Slice the skin and meat. Serve plain or with either plum or hoisin sauce. Serve hot.

紅燒鴨

RED-COOKED DUCK

4 or 5 lb. duck (fresh or frozen)

(a)   1 tbsp. fresh ginger
      2 tbsp. sherry
      2 scallions, chopped

  5 slices ginger
  5 scallions
  ½ tsp. salt

(b) 1½-2 cups soy sauce
     1½-2 cups water

  ½ cup sherry
  ¼ cup sugar
 20 Chinese mushrooms
  4 squares bean curd (each square
     is sliced in half horizontally and
     then into quarters)
  2 tbsp. dried tiger lily stems
  2 tbsp. wood ears

1. Rinse the duck thoroughly and pat dry with paper towels. Rub the duck inside and outside with ingredients (a). Let stand in a cool place for ½-1 hour. Insert the scallions and ginger slices into the stomach cavity of the duck. Pour ingredients (b) into a large pot and add the duck back down, breast up. The sauce should cover at least half the duck.

2. Boil the liquid and then add the sherry. Turn to low heat, cover, and simmer for ½ hour. Then turn the duck over, back up, breast down. Cover and cook another ½ hour on low heat. After Step 2, the duck can be stored in the refrigerator and Step 3 can be continued the next day.

3. Add ¼ cup sugar to the mixture and boil. Turn to low heat, cover, and cook until done (approximately ½ hour).

4. While the duck is cooking, soak the Chinese mushrooms in boiling water for about 15 minutes. Drain and remove the stems. Cut mushroom caps into quarters. Prepare the tiger lily stems and the wood ears by soaking in boiling water for about 15 minutes (separately). Cut the tiger lily stems in half. Combine mushroom quarters, bean curd, tiger lily stems, and wood ears and add to the duck sauce. Cook a few minutes to heat thoroughly and then serve.

宮保鷄丁

CHICKEN CUBELETS

1 young chicken (about 2½ lbs.) or
   1 whole chicken breast (about
   1½ lbs.)

(a) 1½ tbsp. soy sauce
    1½ tbsp. cornstarch

(b) 2 tbsp. soy sauce
    1 tbsp. sherry
    ½ tsp. white vinegar
    1 tsp. sugar
    1 tsp. cornstarch
    ½ tsp. salt (to taste)
    1 tsp. sesame oil

16 pieces small dry red peppers
   about 1-inch length or 12 pieces
   of dry red pepper
 1 tsp. fresh chopped ginger (or ¼
   tsp. ginger powder)
 ½ cup raw skinless peanuts or
   previously fried peanuts
vegetable oil

1. Skin and bone chicken. Remove and discard gristle. Cut the chicken meat
   into ¾-inch cubes. Mix the chicken cubes with ingredients (a) evenly and
   thoroughly. Let the mixture stand for at least ½ hour in the refrigerator.

2. Wash and wipe clean the red peppers. Remove the tips and the seeds. Cut
   into 1-inch pieces. If the peanuts are raw, fry them until golden brown.
   Remove and cool.

3. Heat 4 tbsp. oil in frying pan. When the oil is hot, add the chicken and stir
   well about 1 minute. Remove the chicken from the frying pan.

4. Wash the frying pan and wipe dry. Then add 2 tbsp. oil and fry the red
   peppers until they turn dark. Add ginger and the cubed chicken. Stir
   quickly. Blend ingredients (b) and stir into mixture until thickened and
   heated thoroughly. Turn off the heat. Add peanuts, mix well and serve.

NOTE: If you like it hotter, you can use more dry red peppers or add some
      hot bean paste.

核桃炒鶏片
PARTY CHICKEN

6 large chicken breasts

(a)   2 tbsp. cornstarch
      1 tsp. salt

(b)   1 cup thinly sliced water chestnuts
      1 cup diced bamboo shoots
      2 cups sliced celery
      1 lb. snow peas or green beans (fresh or frozen)

(c)   3 cups chicken broth
      2½ tsp. salt
      2 tsp. monosodium glutamate (optional)
      1 tsp. sugar
      1 tsp. pepper
      6 scallions, cut into 1-inch lengths
      3 slices fresh ginger (if obtainable), cut into strips

(d)   2 tbsp. cornstarch
      2 tbsp. water

1 cup of crisp golden walnut halves
9 tbsp. vegetable or corn oil

1. Skin and bone the chicken breasts. Freeze the chicken; when the chicken begins to thaw, slice it against the grain into thin julienne strips. Rub the chicken with ingredients (a). Let stand in the refrigerator for ½ hour.

2. Saute the chicken strips in 4 tbsp. vegetable oil in a large frying pan over medium high heat for just a few minutes or until the meat turns white. Remove and set aside.

3. Cut the green beans into thin small slivers.

4. Saute 1 cup of walnut halves in 2 tbsp. oil until crisp and golden. Drain and set aside.

5. Heat the remaining 2 tbsp. oil in the frying pan over medium high heat. Add ingredients (b) and stir about ½ minute. Add seasonings mixture (c) and stir a few seconds. Return the chicken meat to the frying pan and stir quickly. Cover and simmer about 5 minutes. Blend ingredients (d) and add to the chicken. Stir constantly until broth is thick and transparent.

6. Serve the chicken, sprinkled with walnuts.

NOTE: This dish is accompanied by cooked rice for a dinner party.

烤鶏

C: 6-8 Servings
W: 3-4 Servings

BROILED CHICKEN

3 lbs. chicken legs

(a) **¼ cup soy sauce**
   1 tbsp. vegetable oil
   ½ tsp. dry mustard
   ¼ tsp. ginger powder or 4 slices of ginger root
   ⅛ tsp. garlic powder or 1 clove garlic, crushed
   dash of black pepper

1. Wash the chicken legs and dry with paper towels.

2. Mix ingredients (a) very well. Dip each chicken leg in the sauce and put it in a big container. Repeat until all the chicken legs are marinated. Pour the leftover sauce over the chicken. Let them soak for several hours or overnight (at least 1 hour). Turn over several times.

3. Put the chicken in a roast pan or on a cookie sheet and place on the middle shelf of the oven. Broil at 350° F for 50 minutes. Check the chicken every 15 minutes, turning over a couple of times. Serve hot or cold.

NOTE: This chicken is good for picnics and barbeques.

香料鷄
FLAVORED STEAM CHICKEN

1 2-3 lb. frying chicken
1 tsp. salt
4 tbsp. vegetable oil
3 scallions, chopped

(a)   6 slices fresh ginger root
       1 tsp. Szechuan peppercorns
       ½ tsp. crushed red pepper

(b)   8 tbsp. soy sauce
       4 tbsp. honey
       ½ tsp. crushed garlic or gar-
       lic chips
       ¼ tsp. salt
       ½ tsp. monosodium gluta-
       mate (optional)

1. Wash the chicken and pat dry with a paper or cloth towel. Rub the inside and outside of the chicken very well with 1 tsp. salt. Let stand for several hours in the refrigerater.

2. Place the chicken in a ovenproof deep bowl which will fit into a big pot with a rack in the bottom or in a regular steamer. Heat the water in the pot until boiling. Put the bowl with the chicken into it. Turn to medium high heat and cover to steam over the boiling water about 15-20 minutes. You must put enough water in the pot for steaming over medium high heat. (If the water is not enough, it may evaporate away and burn the pot as well as the dish.) After 15-20 minutes, turn off the heat. Let the pot stay on the burner for 15 minutes if it is an electric stove. If it is a gas stove, let steam for 20-25 minutes. Then turn off the heat and let stand 15 more minutes. Remove the chicken from the pot and let cool.

3. During the time of steaming, you can prepare the sauce. Heat the 4 tbsp. oil in a frying pan. When the oil is hot, put ingredients (a) into it and stir-fry a few minutes. When the peppercorns turn brown and aromatic, add ingredients (b). Stir about ½ minute. Add the scallions, stir, and remove from the stove. Let cool.

4. Before eating, cut the cold chicken into bite sizes (see Instruction 5 on Meats, chapter 2). Dip each piece into the sauce and arrange them on a serving plate. Serve immediately or keep in the refrigerator until ready to serve.

核桃炒鷄片

Party Chicken (p. 84)

中國烹飪

中國烹飪

熊余文琴著

白切鷄

Salted Chicken (p. 95

中國烹飪

中國烹飪

熊余文琴著

栗子燒鷄

STEWED CHICKEN WITH CHESTNUTS

1 2-3 lb. young chicken
1 lb. chestnuts with outside shell

(a) ¼ cup soy sauce
      3 scallions, cut in half
      3 slices fresh ginger (if obtainable)

(b) ¼ tsp. salt
      2 tbsp. sherry
   ½-¾ cup water
      1 tsp. sugar
      ½ tsp. monosodium glutamate (optional)
      dash of black pepper

4 tbsp. vegetable oil

1. Wash and cut the chicken into 1½-inch chunks (with the bone on). Marinate in ingredients (a) for at least 1 hour.

2. Boil the chestnuts with the shells on over medium high heat. After the water has boiled about 1 or 2 minutes, turn to very low heat and keep the chestnuts in the hot water. Cover to keep them hot. Peel off the shells of the chestnuts while hot. The inner skin of the chestnut will be peeled off with the outside shell. Since the chestnuts are very hot, use a kitchen towel to hold the chestnuts and a knife to break the outside shell. If the water becomes too cool, boil again to facilitate peeling. An alternate method is to peel the outside shells first, then heat the chestnuts over low heat for ½ hour, then peel off the inner skin of the chestnuts. While peeling, keep the remaining chestnuts in the hot water over very low heat.

3. Heat the oil over medium high heat in a heavy pot. When it is hot, put the chicken into it. Stir constantly for 5 minutes until light brown. Then add ingredients (b) and turn to low heat. Stir quickly and thoroughly. Cover tightly and simmer about 15 minutes. Add the chestnuts and cook about 10-15 minutes or until done. If it is not salty enough, salt to taste. Serve hot.

NOTE: This dish can be reheated.

紙包鷄

PAPER WRAPPED CHICKEN

(a) **2 lb. chicken breasts**
¼ cup sherry
¼ cup soy sauce
1 tbsp. sesame oil
2 scallions, chopped
4 slices fresh ginger
¼ tsp. monosodium gluta-
mate (optional)

**1 8 oz. can water chestnuts or 10
fresh ones**
**6 hot red peppers (hot flavoring is
desired), cut into slices**
Chinese parsley (if obtainable)
3 cups vegetable oil
aluminum foil

1. Skin and bone chicken; cut into pieces about 1 by 1 by ½ inches. Marinate chicken in ingredients (a) very well. Let it stand in the refrigerator or a cold place at least one hour.

2. Cut the water chestnuts into slices and set aside.

3. Cut pieces of aluminum foil into 6-inch squares, about 30 pieces.

4.  Place a square of aluminum foil flat with one corner facing you. Put drained chicken pieces in the center and top with 1 strip of red pepper, 1-2 slices of water chestnuts and a sprig of parsley.

Fold the bottom corner near you over the chicken.

 Fold the right point of triangle over to within 3 inches of the left point.

 Fold the left point over to your right so that you fold over the left third of triangle.

 Double the bottom part of the packet toward the top point.

Now you have a tiny envelope with a pointed flap sticking up. Tuck this flap down inside the slot between the folded edges to secure the packet.

5. These packets can be stored in the refrigerator for several hours. Just before serving, heat oil in a deep-fry pot over medium high heat (oil is the right temperature when a cube of bread dropped in the oil forms bubbles). Or you can use an electric deep fryer at 350°F. Fry these packets about 2-3 minutes. Serve immediately.

NOTE: 1. This dish can be kept in the oven for a few minutes without getting tough, but can not be reheated after getting cold.
2. Since each guest opens his or her own package, large paper napkins or hot towels are in order.

紅燒鷄肝

C: 4-6 Servings
W: 1-2 Servings

RED-COOKED CHICKEN LIVERS

1 lb. chicken livers

(a)   4 tbsp. soy sauce
    ¼ cup water
    4 slices fresh ginger root or
    ¼ tsp. ginger powder

1 tsp. sugar
2 tbsp. sherry

1. Wash the livers clean and drain well.

2. Place the ingredients (a) in a deep pot over medium high heat. After the sauce boils, add the chicken livers. When the sauce boils again, add the 2 tbsp. sherry and turn to low heat. Cover and simmer about 20 minutes. Add the 1 tsp. sugar. Cover and simmer another 20 minutes.

3. Uncover and cook at low heat for another 25 minutes.

4. Serve whole or cut into slices. Serve either hot or cold.

醬油鷄

RED COOKED CHICKEN

1 6-7 lb. capon or roasting
   chicken
1 tsp. salt
½ tsp. pepper
2½ cups water
2 cups soy sauce
½ cup sherry
3 scallions, cut in half
5 slices fresh ginger root
2 tbsp. sugar
1 tbsp. sesame oil
1 star anise
   salt to taste

1. Wash and clean the capon inside and outside. Take off the oil sacs and discard. Wipe dry with cloth or paper towels. Rub inside and outside with 1 tsp. salt and ½ tsp. pepper. Let stand at least 1 hour.

2. Insert the scallions and ginger slices into the stomach of the capon. Place the capon, breast up in a big pot. Pour 2 cups soy sauce over the capon. Pour 2½ cups water along the edge of the pot to avoid washing away the soy sauce on the capon. Turn on medium high heat. When the water boils, add the ½ cup sherry. Move the chicken around to avoid it sticking to the bottom of the pot. After the liquid boils again, add the ginger root and the star anise, and turn to low heat. Cover and simmer ½ hour. Check periodically to see if the liquid covers half of the capon; if not, add some hot water. Turn the capon over, add 2 tbsp. sugar and salt to taste. Cover and simmer another ½-1 hour basting frequently. Turn over every ½ hour in between. Use a fork to test the meat on capon breast. If it is tender, it is done.

3. Turn off the heat. Cover and let stand 1-2 hours. Turn the capon over several times. Remove from the pot and brush it with sesame oil. Chill in the refrigerator.

4. Before serving, cut the chicken into 1 x 3-inch chunks (see Instruction 5 on Meat, chapter 2). Arrange on a serving platter. Moisten the chicken with ½ cup of sauce in which it was cooked. Serve cold.

炒鷄片 ·

STIR-FRY CHICKEN SLICES

2 chicken breasts

(a)   **2 tsp. cornstarch**
     ½ tsp. salt

(b)   **1 tbsp. sherry**
     2 tbsp. soy sauce
     1 scallion, chopped
     2 or 3 slices fresh ginger root
     or ¼ tsp. ginger powder

salt to taste
½ lb. fresh mushrooms
¼ lb. can or fresh water chestnuts
¼ lb. can bamboo shoots
5 oz. frozen green peas
¼ lb. dry skinless almonds or walnuts
2 cups vegetable oil

1. Bone and skin chicken breasts. Remove and discard the gristle. Cut against the grain into slices, and rub with ingredients (a) well. Let stand about ½ hour in the refrigerator.

2. Heat the oil till hot. Deep fry almonds about 1 minute. Drain and set aside.

3. Wash the mushrooms and cut vertically into slices. Wash the water chestnuts and bamboo shoots. Cut into small thin slices.

4. Heat 2 tbsp. oil in the frying pan over medium high heat. When the oil is hot, add the chicken. Stir and separate the individual pieces. When the meat changes color, remove and set aside.

5. Heat 2 tbsp. oil in the frying pan over medium high heat. When the oil is hot, add the mushrooms, water chestnuts and bamboo shoots. Stir-fry about 2 minutes. Add ingredients (b) and stir quickly. Return the chicken and stir thoroughly. If not salty enough, salt to taste. Then add the almonds, remove and serve hot.

棒棒鶏

PON PON CHICKEN

1 2½-3 lb. chicken, quartered

(a) 3 tbsp. sesame paste
     3 tbsp. brewed tea

(b) 1 tbsp. hot oil
     ¼ tsp. monosodium gluta-
        mate (optional)
     1 tsp. salt
     2 tsp. sugar
     3 tbsp. chopped scallions
     2½ tbsp. soy sauce
     2 tsp. sesame oil
     1 tbsp. chopped garlic
     1 tsp. white vinegar
     ¼ cup vegetable oil or corn
        oil
     1½ tsp. chili powder

½ cup Szechuan peppercorns
chopped fresh coriander leaves
   (optional)

1. Cook the chicken in a pot with enough water to cover over medium high heat. When the water boils let simmer about 15 minutes or until done. Turn off the heat and let the chicken stand until cool.

2. Stir ingredients (a) in a mixing bowl very well. Add ingredients (b). Stir to blend well. If it is not salty enough, salt to taste.

3. Place the peppercorns in a frying pan and cook over medium heat, stirring and shaking the pan until they are roasted. Then blend the peppercorns in an electric blender until fine. Add 2 tbsp. to the sauce. (The remainder may be kept in a covered container indefinitely.)

4. Pull the meat from the bones of the chicken and cut it into strips. Arrange them on a serving dish and pour the sauce over. Sprinkle with chopped coriander leaves, if available. Serve cold.

NOTE: Toss the chicken and sauce well, before serving.

咖喱鷄

CURRY CHICKEN WITH POTATOES

3½ lb. chicken

(a) 3½ tbsp. curry
    2 cups water

1½ cups sliced onion or a large size
    onion

(b) 3½ tsp. salt
    1 tsp. monosodium gluta-
    mate (optional)

(c) 2 tbsp. cornstarch
    2 tbsp. water

4 tbsp. vegetable oil
3 or 4 potatoes

1. Wash and clean the chicken inside and outside. Pull out excess fat from the cavity of the chicken and discard. Wipe and dry with paper towels. Cut into bite-sized chunks (see Instruction 5 on Meat, chapter 2).

2. Peel the potatoes and cut into 1½-2-inch chunks. Cook in the boiling water about 7-8 minutes over medium heat. Drain and rinse in the cold running water. Drain well and set aside.

3. Heat 4 tbsp. vegetable oil in a big pot over medium high heat. When oil is hot, add the onions. Stir until the onions are light brown. Add mixture (a) and the chicken, stirring quickly until every piece of chicken is evenly coated with curry. When the chicken boils, turn to very low heat. Cover and simmer about 10-15 minutes. Add ingredients (b) stirring and simmering another 10-15 minutes. Then add the potato chunks and simmer another 10 minutes until tender.

4. Blend ingredients (c) into a paste and add to the sauce. Stir constantly until thickened. Serve hot.

NOTE: The dish can be kept warm in the oven and can also be reheated.

炒鶏丁

DICED CHICKEN AND GREEN PEPPERS

1½-2 lb. chicken breast

(a) 1 tbsp. cornstarch
  1 tbsp. sherry
  ½ tsp. salt, or salt to taste
  1 tbsp. soy sauce

¼ cup vegetable oil

(b) 1 large green pepper
  6 water chestnuts
  ¼ lb. fresh mushrooms
  ½ tsp. salt, salt to taste

¼ cup roasted cashews or almonds
2 tbsp. hoisin sauce

1. Bone and skin the chicken breast. Cut the chicken lengthwise into ½-inch strips and cut the strips crosswise to make ½-inch squares. Marinate the chicken with ingredients (a). Let stand at least half an hour in the refrigerator.

2. Wash the green pepper. Remove and discard jthe core and the seeds. Cut the pepper into ½-inch squares. Cut the water chestnuts into ¼-inch cubes and the mushrooms into ¼-inch cubes.

3. Heat 1 tbsp. oil in a frying pan over medium high heat. When the oil is very hot, add ingredients (b). Stir-fry quickly for 2 to 3 minutes. Remove the vegetables and set aside.

4. Pour 3 tbsp. oil into the frying pan over medium high heat. When the oil is very hot (almost smoking), add the chicken meat and separate the individual pieces of chicken. Taste; if not salty enough, salt to taste. After the chicken's color turns white, add the hoisin sauce and stir well. Then add the vegetables and cook about half a minute. Add the cashews or almonds. Heat thoroughly, then place in a serving plate. Serve hot.

白切鷄

SALTED CHICKEN

1 whole chicken, about 2-3 lbs.

(a) 1 tbsp. sherry
1½-2 tsps. salt (to taste)
½ tsp. monosodium gluta-
mate (optional)

3 scallions, cut into 2½-inch
shreds (very thin)
1 tbsp. sesame oil

1. Clean the chicken and pat dry with towels. Rub the inside and outside of the chicken very well with mixture (a). Refrigerate and let stand for at least 4 hours (or overnight). During this time, turn the chicken several times.

2. Place the chicken in a deep ovenproof bowl which will fit on a rack in a big pot (or use a regular steamer). Using high heat, heat water in the pot until boiling. When the water is boiling, put the bowl with the chicken into the pot. Turn to medium high heat and cover. Steam about 15 minutes. *Important:* Do not lift the cover off the pot during the 15 minutes of steaming; otherwise, the time of steaming is not accurate. Remember to put enough water in the pot (about 2 inches deep) to allow for evaporation during steaming. After 15 minutes, if using an electric stove turn off the heat, but let the pot stay on the burner for 10 minutes. If using a gas stove, let steam for 18 minutes, then turn off the heat, and let stand 10 more minutes. Then remove the chicken from the pot and let cool.

3. Save the chicken juice remaining in the bowl. Mix the juice with 1 tbsp. sesame oil. Salt to taste.

4. Chop the chicken into bite-size pieces (see Instruction 5 on Meats, chapter 2). Arrange the pieces of chicken on a serving platter. Sprinkle with the shredded scallions. Pour the chicken juice over the chicken and scallions and serve.

NOTE: The chicken can be kept in the refrigerator until ready to serve.

冬菇鷄

CHICKEN CASSEROLE

1 2-3 lb. chicken

(a) **10 dried Chinese mushrooms**
    20 tiger lily stems
    2 tbsp. wood ears
    2 scallions, minced
    2 slices fresh ginger root or
    ¼ tsp. ginger powder
    3 tbsp. soy sauce
    1 tsp. sugar
    1 tbsp. sherry

  1-1¼ tsp. salt or salt to taste
    1 tsp. sesame oil

1. Wash and clean the chicken inside and outside. Wipe and dry with paper towels. Cut into bite-size chunks (see Instruction 5 on Meats, page 18). Boil about 2 quarts of water. Scald the chicken chunks about 1 minute. Drain under cold running water.

2. Soak the mushrooms, tiger lily stems and wood ears in separate bowls with boiling water for 15-20 minutes. Drain the water. Cut and remove the hard stems of the caps of the mushrooms. Cut each cap into strips. Cut the tiger lily stems into ½ strips if longer. Cut the wood ears into small pieces if too large.

3. Mix the chicken with ingredients (a). Mix well! Let stand a couple of hours. Stir occasionally.

4. Preheat the oven to 375°F. Put the chicken and marinade in a casserole. Place it on the middle shelf of the oven and cook about 45 minutes. Serve hot.

NOTE: You can wrap the chicken in aluminum foil. Put it in a roast pan. Roast at 375°F about 45 minutes.

JELLIED CHICKEN

1 2-3 lb. chicken

(a) 2 scallions, cut into 2-inch
     sections
     3 slices of fresh ginger root

(b) 2 tsp. sherry
     1¾-2 tsp. salt or salt to taste
     1 tsp. monosodium gluta-
     mate (optional)

1 bag of parsley
4 oz. ham, Smithfield ham preferred, sliced
2 packages of unflavored gelatin
6 cups water

1. Wash and clean the chicken inside and outside.

2. Boil 6 cups of water in a big pot over medium high heat. Add ingredients
   (a). After the water boils, put the chicken into the pot. When the water
   boils again, turn to medium heat. Cover and cook about ½ hour. Use a fork
   to test the meat. It is done when it is tender.

3. Remove the chicken from the pot and let cool. Strip off the chicken meat
   with the skin on. Cut the meat into 1- by 1-inch pieces.

4. Boil the chicken broth left in the pot. Dissolve two packages of gelatin in 1
   cup of cold water in a big container. Add 3 cups of boiling chicken broth.
   Stir well. Add the chicken meat and ingredients (b). Mix them well. Taste;
   if not salty enough, salt to taste.

5. Arrange the sliced ham and parsley in a bowl. Pour the chicken mixture
   over it. Put it in the refrigerator until firm.

6. Before serving, invert the bowl over a plate. Run cold water over the bowl
   to loosen the mold onto the plate. Serve cold.

8

SEAFOOD

紅燒魚

RED COOKED FISH

1 2-3 lb. carp, shad, perch, mullet, butterfish, trout, or bass
1 tbsp. sherry
1½ tsp. salt
3 tbsp. flour
6 dried Chinese mushrooms
30 tiger lily stems
¼ cup wood ears

(a) 5 slices fresh ginger or ¼ tsp. ginger powder
     2 cloves garlic or ¼ tsp. garlic powder

3 scallions, cut into 2-inch sections

(b) 3 tbsp. sherry
     4 tbsp. soy sauce
     1 tsp. salt, or salt to taste
     2 cups chicken broth or stock or water
     1 tsp. sugar
     dash of paprika
     ½ tsp. monosodium glutamate (optional)

(c) 2 tbsp. cornstarch
     2 tbsp. water

Vegetable oil (enough for deep-fried fish)

1. Have the fishmonger clean and scale the fish for you, leaving the head on the fish. If possible, ask to have the gills removed from inside the head. Make some diagonal slashes on both sides of the fish. Wipe dry with paper towels. Rub inside and outside of the fish with 1½ tsp. salt. Let stand in the refrigerator about 1 hour.

2. Soak the mushrooms, wood ears, and tiger lily stems in boiling water about 15 to 20 minutes (in separate bowls).

3. Drain the mushrooms, cut off the hard stems and slice the caps. Wash the wood ears and drain. If they are too big, cut into smaller pieces. Wash the tiger lily stems; drain and cut in half if they are too long.

4. After the fish has been in the refrigerator about 1 hour, take out and wipe dry with paper towels and rub it evenly with flour.

5. Pour oil, enough to cover the fish in a deep frying pot, over medium high heat. When the oil is piping hot (almost smoking) slide the fish into the oil; if the fish is too long cut it in half crosswise. Fry about 1 minute. Turn to the other side and fry another 1 minute. Then turn the heat to medium. Fry both sides a total of about 5-6 minutes. Remove the fish to a plate, and put it in the oven to keep warm. Let the oil cool and then drain it through a sieve into a jar. Save the oil for frying fish another time.

6. Fry ingredients (a) with 2 tbsp. oil in a big frying pan over medium high heat and stir quickly. When the oil is hot, add mushrooms, tiger lily stems and wood ears. Stir-fry a few seconds. Add ingredients (b), stir, and return the fish to the pan carefully. Cover and simmer the fish at low heat about 10 minutes. Remove the fish gently to a hot serving platter and leave the sauce in the pan. Keep the fish in warm oven.

7. Heat the sauce over medium high heat. Add the paste of ingredients (c) and stir constantly until thickened. Pour over the fish. Serve immediately.

NOTE: 1. If the oil is not piping hot, the fish will stick to the bottom of the pan.
2. If you do not have enough oil to cover the fish when you deep-fry it, you can spoon oil over the top of the fish. Continue to do so, and after 1-2 minutes turn the fish. Continue cooking another 2 minutes. Turn to medium heat and continue to cook again. The time will be a bit longer because you have to turn the fish over twice.

FRIED WHITING FISH

3 or 4 lbs. whiting fish, cleaned and scaled

(a)   5 slices ginger root
      5 scallion stalks
      ¼ tsp. garlic powder
      4 tbsp. soy sauce
      2 tbsp. sherry
      4 tbsp. chicken broth
      1 tsp. salt
      1½ tsp. sugar

some flour

(b) 20 tiger lily stems
      ¼ cup bamboo strips
      3 tbsp. wood ears

(c)   1 tsp. cornstarch
      1 tbsp. water

½ tsp. monosodium glutamate (optional)
1 cup vegetable or corn oil

1. Wash the whitings and dry with paper towels. Make a few slashes crosswise on each side of the fish. Rub with the mixture of ingredients (a). Marinate for 8-10 hours or overnight in the refrigerator (the longer, the better).

2. Soak the tiger lily stems and wood ears in separate bowls for about 15-20 minutes. Cut the tiger lily stems into halves if too long.

3. Lift up and drain the remaining sauce off of the whitings and save the sauce. Rub the whitings with some flour.

4. Heat the oil over medium high heat on an electric stove or over high heat on a gas stove (until very hot, almost smoking). Add the fish and cook one side about 5 minutes. Then turn over and cook until done, about 5 minutes.

NOTE: Save the oil used in frying this fish for reuse another time. (See General Instruction 7, chapter 2.)

5. Put the fish on a heated platter in a warm oven. Cook the sauce with 2 tbsp. chicken broth and ingredients (b). Stir and add salt to taste. Then add the blended mixture (c). Stir until thickened. Pour over the fish and serve.

蒸鰵魚

C: 4-5 Servings
W: 2-3 Servings

STEAMED FILLET OF HADDOCK

1 lb. fillet of haddock
1 clove garlic, minced
1 or 2 tbsp. dry fermented black beans

(a) 1 tbsp. dry sherry
     2 tbsp. soy sauce
     ½ tsp. sugar
     1 tsp. oil
     3 slices fresh ginger root, shredded
     1 tsp. monosodium glutamate (optional)
     ½ tsp. paprika

3 scallions, cut into 2-inch sections
3 pieces bacon or sliced pork fat

1. Soak the black beans with 3 tbsp. hot water for 10-15 minutes. Crush the black beans together with minced garlic. Add to ingredients (a). Mix and set aside.

2. Place the fillet of haddock in a shallow heatproof dish, which is fitted in a deep pan used as a steamer (see chapter 1). Sprinkle the mixture (a) over the fish with a spoon. Cover with the bacon or pork fat. Put the dish into the deep steamer with about two inches of water. Cover and turn to high heat. When the water boils, turn to medium heat and steam about 15-18 minutes until done.

3. Remove the dish from the steamer. Take away the bacon or pork fat. Garnish with scallions. Serve hot.

101

STEAMED WHITING FISH

2-3 lbs. whiting (about 5 medium size whiting fish)

1½ tsp. salt

1 clove garlic or ¼ tsp. garlic powder

3 tbsp. dry fermented black beans (optional)

(a) 3 tbsp. soy sauce

1 tsp. sugar

1 tbsp. oil

3 or 4 slices fresh ginger root, shredded

1 tsp. paprika

1 tsp. monosodium glutamate (optional)

3 scallions, cut into 2-inch sections

1. Soak the black beans with 3 tbsp. hot water for 10 to 15 minutes. Crush the black beans with minced garlic (or garlic powder). Add to ingredients (a). Set the mixture aside.

2. Have the fishmonger clean the whiting fish, retaining the heads and tails. Wash and clean the fish. Dry with paper towels. Make three diagonal slashes on both sides of each fish. Rub them inside and outside with the 1½ tsp. salt thoroughly. Let stand in the refrigerator at least ½ hour.

3. Place the fish in a shallow heatproof bowl or dish which fits into a deep pot used as a steamer (see chapter 1). Sprinkle ingredients (a) over the fish with a spoon. Put the dish in the steamer with about 2 inches of water. Cover and turn to high heat. When the water boils, turn to medium heat and steam about 20-25 minutes or until done.

4. Remove the dish from the steamer. Garnish with scallions. Serve hot.

乾噴蝦

SPLASHED SHRIMP

1½ lbs. large fresh shrimp

(a) 1 tbsp. sherry
2 tbsp. soy sauce

3 or 4 scallions, cut into 2-inch sections
3 or 4 slices ginger root

(b) 2 tbsp. soy sauce
1 tbsp. sugar
2 tbsp. ketchup
¼ tsp. salt
¼ tsp. monosodium glutamate (optional)
4 tbsp. chicken broth or stock

(c) 1 tsp. cornstarch
1 tbsp. water

1. Do not shell the shrimp, but use a pair of kitchen scissors and cut off the small feelers on the underside. Devein by cutting open a small section of the back and pulling the vein out with a skewer or a toothpick.

2. In a mixing bowl, place the shrimp and add seasonings (a). Mix well and let stand ½ hour.

3. Heat 4 tbsp. oil in a large frying pan over medium high heat. Add the scallions and the ginger. Stir-fry quickly. When the oil is very hot, add the shrimp. Stir-fry about one to two minutes until the color changes. Add ingredients (b). Stir, then cover and cook another couple of minutes. Add the mixture paste (c). Stir quickly until the liquid thickens.

4. Serve hot or cold.

NOTE: This dish may be stored in the refrigerator and served cold.

肉汁蝦仁

SHRIMP WITH MEAT SAUCE

1 lb. shrimp, shelled and deveined
5 tbsp. vegetable oil
¼ lb. lean ground pork

(a) 1 tbsp. cornstarch
     1 tsp. sherry

dash of salt

(b) 1 beaten egg
     1 scallion, finely chopped
     2 tbsp. soy sauce
     5 slices fresh ginger
     2 tbsp. sherry
     ½ tsp. salt
     1½ tsp. fermented black beans
     ½ tsp. sugar
        dash of garlic powder
     ¼ tsp. pepper
     ½ cup chicken broth or stock

(c) 1 tsp. cornstarch
     2 tbsp. water

½ tsp. baking soda

1. Soak the black fermented beans for 15 minutes in ¼ cup boiling water and crush them into the water.

2. Mix ½ tsp. baking soda with water in a bowl. Stir the shrimp in the mixture for 2 minutes and pour the water away (this enhances the crispness of the shrimp). Wash and clean the shrimp and put the shrimp in cold running water. Drain well and wipe dry with paper towels. Then rub with ingredients (a) very well.

3. Heat 3 tbsp. oil in a frying pan over medium high heat. When the oil is very hot (almost smoking), add the shrimp and stir quickly. Add a dash of salt and stir until the shrimp changes color. Remove and set aside.

4. Heat the remaining oil in the frying pan over medium high heat. When the oil is hot, add the ground pork. Stir and fry quickly, separating the pork pieces. When the color of the meat changes pour ingredients (b) into it. Stir

quickly about 1 minute. Return the shrimp to the pan. Stir and heat thoroughly. Then mix ingredients (c) into a paste, and pour into the pan. Stir constantly until thickened. Serve hot.

蕃茄汁炒蝦

C: 4-6 Servings
W: 3-4 Servings

SHRIMP WITH KETCHUP

1 lb. medium-sized shrimp
1 tsp. cornstarch
2 tbsp. sherry

(a) 1 tsp. minced ginger root
3 or 4 stalks chopped scallions
4 tbsp. ketchup
1-2 chopped hot peppers
1 tsp. soy sauce
1 tsp. salt
¼ cup chicken broth

(b) 2 tsp. cornstarch
2 tsp. water

4 tbsp. vegetable oil

1. Shell and devein the shrimp (see Instruction 1 on Seafood, chapter 2). Leave the tails on. Wipe the shrimp and dry with paper towels. Mix well with 1 tsp. cornstarch.

2. Heat the oil in the frying pan over medium high heat (if electric range). When the oil is very hot, add the shrimp, stir and add sherry. Stir-fry until the color of the shrimp changes. Remove the shrimp and save the oil in the pan. Add ingredients (a) and stir well. Then blend ingredients (b) and add to the sauce. Stir until it thickens. Add the cooked shrimp and stir thoroughly. Pour over a heated platter and serve hot.

蝴蝶蝦
BUTTERFLY SHRIMP

24 large shrimp (about 3 inches in length)

(a) 2 tsp. sherry
¼-½ tsp. salt or to taste
¼ tsp. pepper

(b) 1 level cup flour
½ cup cornstarch
1 tsp. baking powder
2 tbsp. beaten eggs
1 cup water (if too thick, add
1-2 tbsp. more)
2 tsp. oil

4 cups of vegetable oil

(c) 1 tbsp. vegetable oil
2 tbsp. horseradish
½ cup water
1 tbsp. soy sauce
2 tbsp. vinegar
salt to taste
4 tbsp. sugar
1 tbsp. cornstarch
½ tsp. paprika

1. Peel the shells and devein the shrimp, leaving the tip of the tails intact. Rinse the shrimp well and pat dry with paper towels. Rub the shrimp with ingredients (a). Let stand about 1 hour in the refrigerator.

2. Blend ingredients (b) into a smooth batter, but not watery.

3. Mix ingredients (c) into a sauce and heat until thickened. Keep warm in the oven.

4. Heat 4 cups of oil in a deep fryer or deep pot. The right temperature is reached when bubbles form on a piece of bread. Dip the shrimp into the batter one at a time (keeping the tips of the tails free of batter). Clamp the batter-coated shrimp at the tail with chopsticks or ice tongs and hold in the oil for ½ minute before dropping it into the oil (This prevents the shrimp from sticking to the bottom or sides of the pot). Fry until golden brown and crispy. As the shrimp are cooking, keep the finished shrimp warm in the oven.

5. Serve the sauce along with the shrimp (as a dip).

NOTE: The shrimp can also be served with other sauces, such as mustard sauce.

炒大蝦

STIR-FRY SHRIMP CURLS

1 lb. medium to jumbo shrimp

(a)   **1 tbsp. sherry**
      ½ tsp. salt

(b)   **3 tbsp. chicken broth or any stock**
      3½ tsp. sugar
      1 tsp. vinegar
      6 scallions, cut into 2-inch sections
      1 clove garlic, crushed
      2 slices ginger
      1 tsp. pepper
      ¼ tsp. salt, or salt to taste

(c)   **1 tsp. cornstarch**
      ½ tsp. soy sauce
      ½ tsp. water

4 tbsp. vegetable oil

1. Devein the shrimp. Leave the shells and tails on. Wash the shrimp and drain thoroughly. Wipe dry with paper towels.

2. Heat the oil in a frying pan over medium high heat. When the oil is very hot (almost smoking), add the shrimp into it. Stir quickly about ½ minute, add ingredients (a) and stir constantly. When the shrimp changes color, add ingredients (b). Keep on stirring the shrimp about 4 to 5 minutes. Add the paste ingredients (c). Braise shrimp about 1 minute or until done. Serve hot.

青豆蝦仁

SHRIMP WITH PEAS

12 oz. uncooked shrimp, shelled and deveined
1 lb. frozen green peas
¼ cup diced bamboo shoots
2 tbsp. chicken broth
1 tbsp. sherry
½ tsp. salt or salt to taste
1 tbsp. cornstarch
3 slices ginger root
2 scallions, cut into 2-inch sections
4 tbsp. vegetable oil
¼ tsp. monosodium glutamate (optional)
1 tsp. sugar

1. Pour 2 tbsp. oil in a frying pan over medium high heat. When the oil is hot, add the peas and bamboo shoots. Stir for a few seconds. Add ½ tsp. salt, or salt to taste. Stir and add monosodium glutamate. Stir-fry for a couple of minutes until done. Remove and set aside.

2. Wash the shrimp and drain well. Dry them with paper towels. Rub them with 1 tbsp. cornstarch.

3. Pour the remaining 2 tbsp. oil into the frying pan over medium high heat. Add the ginger root and scallions. Stir-fry for a few seconds. When the oil is piping hot (almost smoking), add the shrimp. Stir for a few seconds and add the 1 tbsp. sherry and ½ tsp. salt. Stir until the shrimp changes color. Remove and discard the ginger and scallions. Return the peas and bamboo shoots to the mixture in the pan. Stir and add the sugar. If not salty enough, salt to taste. Remove from the heat and place on a warm serving platter. Serve immediately.

蟹肉炒白菜

CRABMEAT WITH CELERY CABBAGE

1 cup cooked crabmeat (or 1 7-oz.
   can crabmeat)
2 lb. Chinese celery cabbage
1 tbsp. ginger root, chopped
1 tbsp. scallions, chopped
1 tbsp. sherry

(a)   4 tbsp. chicken   broth   or
      chicken stock
      1 tsp. salt

(b)   1 cup chicken broth
      ¼ tsp. salt

(c)   1 tbsp. cornstarch
      1 tbsp. water

6 tbsp. vegetable oil or corn oil

1. Wash the cabbage. Cut into half lengthwise and then into 2-inch sections crosswise. Separate the white stems and green leaves.

2. Heat 2 tbsp. oil in a large frying pan over medium high heat. When the oil is hot, place the cabbage stems into it. Stir quickly a couple of minutes. Then add the leaves and ingredients (a). Stir and cover about 2 minutes. Then uncover and cook another 2 minutes until crispy. Place in a bowl and keep in a warm oven.

3. Heat the remaining oil in the frying pan over medium high heat. Fry the scallions and ginger a few seconds. Add the crabmeat and splash with sherry. Stir-fry ½ minute. Add ingredients (b) and fry another ½ minute. Add the paste ingredients (c) and stir constantly until the sauce thickens.

4. With perforated ladle place the cabbage on a platter (do not use the soup stock from the cabbage). Pour the crabmeat with sauce mixture over the cabbage. Serve hot.

NOTE: Cauliflower, asparagus, broccoli or Chinese ''bok choy'' can be used in place of the celery cabbage if you prefer.

炒龍蝦

STIR-FRY LOBSTERS
(Cantonese style)

2 lb. lobsters or lobster tails
¼ lb. ground pork
1 crushed garlic clove

(a) 1½ tbsp. black fermented beans
   1 crushed garlic clove
   3 tbsp. soy sauce
   ½ tsp. sugar
   ½ cup boiling water
   ½ tsp. salt
   2 tbsp. sherry
   1 scallion, chopped fine

(b) 2 tbsp. water
   1 tbsp. cornstarch

1 egg, lightly beaten
4 tbsp. vegetable oil

1. Soak the black fermented beans in ¼ cup hot water for 15-20 minutes. Crush and add to ingredients (a).

2. Cut the lobsters or lobster tails into 1½-inch chunks (see Instruction 6 on Seafood, chapter 2).

3. Heat 4 tbsp. oil in a large frying pan over medium high heat. When the oil is hot, add the garlic and the ground pork. Brown quickly and separate into small pieces. Then remove the garlic and add the lobster chunks and ingredients (a). Stir well. Cover the pan and cook about 7-10 minutes. (The tougher lobsters take longer time. Even though lobsters of different sizes are cut to pieces of the same size, the meat of larger lobsters should be cooked longer.) When the lobster chunks are done, add the paste of ingredients (b). Stir constantly until the sauce thickens and coats the lobster chunks. Then add the beaten egg. Heat and stir until the egg sets. Serve immediately.

NOTE: If not salty enough, salt to taste.

蒸蚌

STEAMED CLAMS

3 dozen clams
¼ cup salt

Sauce for dip:
2 tbsp. soy sauce
1 tsp. sherry
2 scallions, chopped very fine
3 slices fresh ginger, chopped
very fine
1 tsp. sesame oil
2 tsp. sugar
½ tsp. white vinegar

1. Wash the shell of each individual clam with a brush. Put the clams in a basin of cold water. Add salt and mix well. Let stand about 5-6 hours. Drain the clams and rinse individually under running water.

2. Put the clams in a clam steamer or a regular steamer with a perforated inner bottom. Cover and heat the water to boiling and steam for 5-6 minutes over medium high heat until the bivalves open.

3. Mix the sauce well. Serve immediately.

9

NOODLES, RICE, AND EGGS

布羅可里肉絲麵

C: 6-8 Servings
W: 3-4 Servings

PORK STRIPS AND BROCCOLI
STEMS WITH NOODLES

½ lb. lean pork loin or butt (increase amount of pork according to amount of fat present—½ lb. of pork strips is needed)
1 bunch broccoli
½ lb. fresh mushrooms
5 scallions (cut into 2-inch sections)

(a) 2½ tbsp. soy sauce
1 tsp. sherry
½ tsp. sugar
¼ tsp. sesame oil
dash of ginger powder
dash of garlic powder
1 tbsp. cornstarch

8 oz. Chinese noodles or very thin spaghetti
½ cup chicken broth or stock
½ tsp. salt or to taste
½ tsp. monosodium glutamate (optional)

(b) 2 tsp. cornstarch
4 tbsp. water

5 tbsp. vegetable or corn oil

1. Cut across the grain of partially frozen meat into thin slices. Cut each slice into strips. Marinate the meat strips with ingredients (a). Mix well and let stand in the refrigerator for at least ½ hour.

2. Pinch off the broccoli flower tips and save for cooking vegetable dishes. Peel off the skins of the stems. Then cut stems into slices and then shreds, about 3½-4 cups. Wash mushrooms and cut into slices.

3. Boil the noodles about 4-5 minutes and drain. Rinse a few minutes in cold running water and place on a baking sheet (If using spaghetti, boil about 8-10 minutes, drain, and rinse under cold running water). Mix noodles with 1 tbsp. vegetable oil and set aside. Before serving, heat the noodles in the oven at 150-200° F for 15-20 minutes.

4. Heat 3 tbsp. vegetable oil in the frying pan over medium high heat. When the oil is hot, add the meat strips and stir quickly, separating the shreds. After the meat loses its red color, stir for a minute and remove from the pan. Heat the remaining oil in the pan. When the oil is hot, add the broccoli shreds and scallions. Cook about ½ minute, and then pour ½ cup of chicken broth into mixture. Stir and then add mushrooms. Cook another ½ minute. Add ½ tsp. salt and ½ tsp. monosodium glutamate. Stir thoroughly. Return the meat to the pan. Blend ingredients (b) and pour into the pan. Stir constantly until the sauce is thickened.

5. Place the heated noodles in a warm deep serving platter. Pour pork and vegetable sauce over. Serve immediately.

NOTE: This is also a good dish for lunch.

炸醬麵

C: 4 Servings
W: 4 Servings

NOODLES WITH MEAT SAUCE

1 lb. boneless pork butt or shoulder ham (ground only once)

(a) 2 tbsp. sherry
½ cup cooked green peas (frozen or fresh)
2 chopped scallions
4 tbsp. hoisin sauce
¾ tsp. salt or salt to taste
1 tsp. sugar

¼ cup chicken broth
1 large cucumber
2 cloves chopped garlic
3 scallions, cut in 2-inch sections and finely shredded
1 lb. fresh Chinese noodles or very thin spaghetti
3 tbsp. vegetable oil or corn oil

1. Peel the cucumber and cut in half lengthwise. Scoop out and discard the seeds. Cut the cucumber into thin strips (⅛" x ⅛" x 2").

2. Put the cucumber strips, garlic and scallions on a plate.

3. Heat 2 tbsp. oil in a frying pan over medium high heat. When the oil is hot, add the ground pork. Stir quickly for a few minutes until the meat browns lightly. Add ingredients (a) and mix well. Pour in the chicken broth. Bring to a boil and cook rapidly over medium heat for about 5 to 6 minutes. Stir constantly until the broth evaporates. Turn off the heat. Cover to keep warm.

4. Bring 2 quarts of water to boil over medium high heat. Add the noodles. Stir occasionally to prevent sticking. Cook about 5 or 6 minutes. Drain through a colander and put in a warm serving platter. Toss the noodles with 1 tbsp. oil. If using thin spaghetti, cook according to the package instructions.

5. Serve the noodles with the meat sauce, cucumber, garlic and scallions mixed together.

NOTE: 1. If you like a hot flavor, you can add some hot sauce (see index).
2. This is a good dish for picnics.

牛肉炒飯

BEEF AND BROCCOLI
WITH RICE

1 lb. flank steak
1 bunch broccoli
6 tbsp. vegetable oil
1 tsp. salt or salt to taste

(a)   4 tbsp. soy sauce
     2 tbsp. sherry
     1 tsp. sugar
     ½ tsp. sesame oil
      dash of ginger powder
      dash of garlic powder
   1½ tbsp. cornstarch

2 cups rice (long grain)

1. Trim the gristle and fat from the meat and discard. Cut the flank steak against the grain into slices. Marinate the meat in ingredients (a). Let stand at least ½ hour.

2. Pinch off the broccoli flower and save stems for other recipes (see note). Cut into half if too long. Wash them under cold running water and drain.

3. Heat 2 tbsp. oil in a frying pan over medium high heat. Sprinkle salt over the oil. When the oil is hot, add the broccoli flower branches. Stir about ½ minute and add the chicken broth. Stir and cover about 2 or 3 minutes. Stir occasionally until tender and crunchy. Remove from the pan and set aside.

4. Wash the rice in a pot. With 3 cups of water, cover the rice. When the water boils, turn to low heat. Cover and simmer about 16 to 18 minutes or until done. Keep warm.

5. Heat the remaining oil in the pan over medium high heat. When the oil is very hot, stir the beef slices into it. Separate each slice individually, about 1 or 2 minutes until the meat color changes. Then return the broccoli to the pan and stir quickly.

6. Place the boiled rice in a serving plate. Pour the beef and broccoli over the rice. Serve immediately.

NOTE: The broccoli stems can be used in recipe "Pork Strips and Broccoli Stems with Noodles" (see index).

ROAST PORK AND EGG RICE

4 **eggs**
8 **cups cooked rice (cold)**
½ **cup fresh or frozen green peas**
½ **cup chopped onion or scallion**

(a) ¾ **tsp. salt**
   1 **tsp. sherry**
   ½ **tsp. monosodium gluta-**
      mate (optional)

½ **tsp. salt**
1 **cup bean sprouts**
1 **cup diced celery**
2 **cups diced roast pork**

(b) 2 **tbsp. soy sauce**
   ½ **tsp. salt, or salt to taste**

½ **cup water chestnuts (from can,**
   about 15-20)
6 **tbsp. vegetable oil**

1. Beat eggs and mix with ingredients (a).

2. If the green peas are fresh, cook in the boiled water for 5-10 minutes or until tender. Then drain under running cold water. Set aside. If they are frozen peas, you need only to defrost them or cook according to the package directions. Set aside.

3. Heat 2 tbsp. of oil in a frying pan over medium high heat. When the oil is hot add the egg mixture. Stir and break the scrambled eggs into small pieces. Remove and set aside.

4. Heat another 1 tbsp. oil in the frying pan. When the oil is hot, add salt, the celery, onion, bean sprouts and peas. Stir about 1 or 2 minutes until done. Set aside.

5. Pour the remaining oil in the pan over medium heat. When the oil is hot, add the cold rice. Stir quickly and separate the rice individually by turning, stirring, scrambling lightly without messing up the rice. Add ingredients (b). When the rice is warm, add the eggs and all the ingredients (meat and vegetables). Stir thoroughly. If not salty enough, salt to taste. Heat thoroughly and serve hot.

NOTE: Use "long grain" for cooked rice. Use 1 cup of rice with 1¾ cups water. Bring to boil over high heat. Reduce heat to low. Cover and simmer about 16-18 minutes or until the water is absorbed. In this recipe use about 4 cups of uncooked rice. After the rice is cooked, spread it over a big plate, and let cool.

煮飯

BOILED RICE

1 cup white rice
1½-1¾ cups cold water

1. Place the rice in a deep pot with 2 quarts of water. Stir and rinse the rice thoroughly. Drain the rice well. Pour 1½ cups cold water into the pot over medium high heat. When the water boils, turn to very low heat and cover tightly. If the rice is too dry, add ¼ cup more water. Simmer about 16 to 18 minutes. Turn off the heat, but do not uncover the pot. Let stand for a few minutes. Then remove the cover and fluff the rice with a chopstick or fork. Serve the rice while it is hot.

2. If the rice must wait, keep it in a heatproof serving bowl in a preheated oven at 200°-250° F.

NOTE: 1. Leftover rice can be reheated by putting into a pot with a little water over very low heat. Cover and cook about ½ hour depending on how much rice you have.
2. There are some very good electric rice cookers made in the Orient. They are simple to operate and are fully automatic. Once the rice and water are added to the cooker, the rice has been started and can be forgotten while you concentrate on the dishes to be cooked (with all the burners available since the rice is cooking in its own pot). Cooking time is about 20-30 minutes depending on the amount of rice.

鹹蛋
SALTED EGGS

20-24 large eggs
   7 cups water
  ¾ cup and 2 tbsp. salt

1. Dissolve ¾ cup salt in 7 cups water in a big porcelain or Pyrex container.

2. Put 20-24 eggs in it. Sprinkle 2 tbsp. salt on the top of the eggs. The salt water should cover the eggs.

3. Cover and keep them at 64°-68° F for 5 to 6 weeks or at 70° F or higher for 4 to 5 weeks. The warmer the temperature, the less time you need for salting the eggs.

4. Transfer the eggs to an egg box or bowl. They can be stored in the refrigerator for 3 or 4 weeks.

5. When you need to cook them, put in a deep pot with enough water to cover over low heat. Cook until done. (In low heat, the eggs will not crack.) Cut into half, quarter, or eight wedges. Serve hot or cold.

NOTE: You can cook salted eggs with ground pork; see index for "Pork with Salted Eggs."

青豆蝦仁

Shrimp with Snow Peas (p. 108)

中國烹飪

中國烹飪

熊余文琴 著

布羅可里肉絲麵

中國烹飪

**Pork Strips and Brocolli
Stems with Noodles (p. 112)**

中國烹飪

熊余文琴 著

鶏粥

CHICKEN CONGEE

(a) 6 pieces of dried bean curd
        (pinched into small pieces)
2 or 3 chicken bones
      ¼ cup gingko nuts (optional)
      ¼ cup fresh peanuts

(b)   2 oz. chicken meat slices
        2 oz. pork slices

  2 tsp. cornstarch
  ½ cup plain rice
  ¼ cup glutinous rice
  8 cups water
  1 cup chopped lettuce
1½ tsp. salt or salt to taste

1. Wash both kinds of rice, and put into a deep pot. Add 3 cups of water and ingredients (a) over medium high heat. When the water boils, turn to low heat and cook about 1 hour until done. (This is the congee.)

2. Mix the cornstarch with the chicken slices and pork slices (1 tsp. cornstarch for each). Set aside.

3. When the congee is ready, add ingredients (b) and salt. Stir and cook for several minutes. Taste; if not salty enough, salt to your taste.

4. Before serving, add the chopped lettuce and mix well. It will be crispy and tasty.

119

揚州炒飯

YANG CHOW FRIED RICE

C. 6-8 Servings
W: 4-5 Servings

8 cups of cooked rice (cold)
4 eggs
4 oz. chicken meat
4 oz. green peas
4 oz. roast pork or ham
4 oz. shrimp, shelled and deveined
6 scallions, minced
15 water chestnuts (canned), diced
1 cup bamboo shoots, diced
vegetable or corn oil

(a) ¼ tsp. salt or salt to taste
     ½ tsp. sherry

(b) ¼ tsp. salt or salt to taste
     dash of pepper
     1 tsp. cornstarch

(c) dash of pepper
     ¼ tsp. salt
     ½ tsp. sherry

(d) 1 tbsp. soy sauce
     ½ tsp. salt or salt to taste

1. "Long grain" rice is the best rice for cooking fried rice. Cook the rice and let it cool before frying (If in a hurry, the rice can be put in the refrigerator to cool). Separate the grains of rice before frying.

2. Beat the eggs very well with ingredients (a).

3. Cut the chicken meat into dices. Mix thoroughly with ingredients (b).

4. Dry the shrimp with paper towels and cut into dices. Toss shrimp with ingredients (c). Mix well.

5. Parboil the green peas in salted boiling water about 2 or 3 minutes. Rinse in cold water and drain well.

6. Heat 1 tbsp. oil in the frying pan over medium high heat. Add a dash of salt to the oil. When the oil is hot, add the bamboo shoots. Stir quickly about ½ minute. Remove from pan and set aside.

120

7. With the same pan, heat 3 tbsp. oil over medium high heat. When the oil is hot, pour the beaten eggs into it. Swing the pan in a circular motion. Use a spatula to stir the egg. When the eggs start to firm, remove the pan from the heat. Stir quickly just like scrambled eggs, but separate the eggs into fine pieces. Remove and set aside.

8. Heat 1 tbsp. oil in the frying pan. When the oil is hot, add the chicken dices. Stir quickly. When the meat changes color, remove and set aside.

9. Heat 2 tbsp. oil in the same frying pan. When the oil is hot, add the shrimp. Stir a few seconds and pour ½ tsp. sherry over the shrimp. Stir, separating the pieces of shrimp. When the shrimp turns pink, remove and set aside.

10. Heat the remaining oil (2 tbsp. oil) in the pan over medium high heat. When the oil is hot, add the cold cooked rice. Stir constantly until warm. Add ingredients (d). Stir-fry quickly. Salt to taste if needed. Keep on stirring for a few minutes. Then add all the ingredients and mix thoroughly. Stir until everything is hot. Remove to heated ovenproof casserole. Serve hot.

芙蓉蛋

EGG FOO YUNG

4 to 5 eggs

(a)   1 lb. or 1½ lbs. chopped cooked chicken, shrimp, pork, turkey or crabmeat
   8 Chinese dried mushrooms or 1-8 oz. can button mushrooms
   ½ stalk celery, chopped (or ¾ stalk celery if it is small.)
   ½ cup diced bamboo shoots
   ½ cup diced water chestnuts
   1 can drained bean sprouts
   1¼ tsp. salt or salt to taste
   ½ tsp. pepper

10 tbsp. vegetable oil or corn oil

Brown sauce (gravy):

(b) 1½ tbsp. cornstarch
   1 tbsp. soy sauce
   1¾ cups cold chicken broth
   ¼ tsp. sugar
   dash of salt
   dash of pepper

1. Soak the Chinese dried mushrooms in boiling water for 15 minutes. Squeeze out the water in the mushrooms. Cut away the hard part of stems from the caps, and chop each of the caps into shreds. If you use the button mushrooms, just cut each into shreds.

2. Beat eggs slightly. Add all ingredients (a). Mix them very well.

3. Cover the bottom of an 8-inch frying pan with 2 to 3 tbsp. oil over medium heat. When the oil is hot, pour ¼ of the mixture into the frying pan and cook the mixture (like an omelet) until brown on one side. (If you like smaller pieces, you can divide the mixture into 8 parts.) Turn carefully and cook until brown on the other side. Repeat until the mixture is done.

4. Make brown sauce: Combine ingredients (b) in a frying pan. Cook and stir over medium heat until the mixture comes to a boil and thickens. Serve egg foo yung with brown gravy sauce.

紅燒肉湯麵

NOODLES WITH RED COOKED PORK

1 lb. boneless pork butt or tenderloin
1½ qts. cold water
¼ cup sherry
6 tbsp. soy sauce
2 tbsp. sugar
1 lb. Chinese egg noodles or ¾ box of very thin spaghetti (such as San Giorgie No. 11 spaghetti)
2 tbsp. vegetable oil
1 tsp. salt
½ tsp. monosodium glutamate (optional)
2 lb. celery cabbage

1. Cut the meat into about 1½-inch chunks. Scald the meat in boiling water about 2 minutes. Then rinse with cold water and drain.

2. Put the meat in a pot. Add the water and soy sauce. Bring to boil over medium high heat. Add the sherry and turn to low heat. Cover and simmer about 30 minutes. Taste the sauce; if it is not salty enough, add ¼ tsp. salt or salt to taste. Add the sugar. Cover and simmer on very low heat (or on *warm* if it is an electric range) about ½ hour or until the meat is tender.

3. Boil the Chinese noodles 4 to 6 minutes or until tender (or cook the spaghetti 7 minutes for medium and 10 minutes for well done).

4. Wash the cabbage leaves. Cut into 3-inch length sections. Separate the stems and leaves. Heat 2 tbsp. oil in a frying pan over medium high heat. When the oil is hot, put the cabbage stems into the oil. Stir and cover. Cook about 3 minutes. Add the salt and the cabbage leaves. Stir quickly and cover to cook about 1 or 2 minutes. Add the monosodium glutamate. If not salty enough, salt to taste. Stir and remove from heat.

5. Put the boiled noodles in bowls, while still hot. Put the meat chunks, sauce and the cabbage over the noodles. Serve hot.

NOTE: 1. This is a good meal for lunch. You can cook the red cooked pork the previous night. Before serving, boil the noodles and cook the cabbage. Heat the meat. Your lunch will be ready in 15-20 minutes.
2. Any vegetable can be substituted for the celery cabbage.

123

蛋 捲

EGG DUMPLINGS

1 lb. ground pork

(a) 1½ tsp. minced fresh ginger
     root (if obtainable) or ¼
     tsp. ginger powder
  3 scallions, chopped finely
  4 tbsp. soy sauce
  ½ tsp. salt
  2 tbsp. sherry
1½ tsp. sugar
  ½ tsp. monosodium gluta-
     mate (optional)
1½ tbsp. cornstarch
  3 tbsp. water

4 tbsp. vegetable or corn oil
7 eggs
2 lb. celery cabbage

(b) 1½ cups chicken broth
  ½ tsp. salt or salt to taste

1. Mix the ground pork with ingredients (a). Blend well with your fingers. Let stand at least ½ hour. This is the pork filling.

2. Beat the eggs with a fork or chopstick until well blended. Set aside.

3. Wash the celery cabbage and cut each big leaf lengthwise into two parts. Then cut each part into about 2-inch sections and set aside.

4. Make the dumpling skins: Use a 10-inch frying pan (a Teflon pan is best). Brush with vegetable oil over medium heat. When the pan is hot, turn the heat to low. Pour about 5 to 5½ tbsp. of the beaten egg into a small cup. While turning the pan in a circular motion, pour the eggs slowly from the cup into the pan until a thin and round egg skin forms (about 8-inches in diameter). If there are a few spots without egg in the skin, fill them with a few drops of uncooked beaten egg. Then put the pan on low heat and cook about 2-3 minutes. When the cake is firm, lift it up carefully with a spatula or your fingers and remove to a plate. Repeat the same procedure and make another cake. Do not pile the skins together since they might stick together. Store each skin separately. With the beaten egg mixture, 8 egg cake skins can be made. Any uncooked egg leftover can be used for sealing the edges of egg dumplings.

5. Divide the pork filling into 8 equal parts. Spread the filling evenly on the skin. Do not put near the edge of the skin. Roll it gently and seal the edges with a little beaten egg. Press the edges together firmly to make them adhere. Continue until all the skins have been filled. (See illustrations.)

1

Spread the meat filling over the egg skin

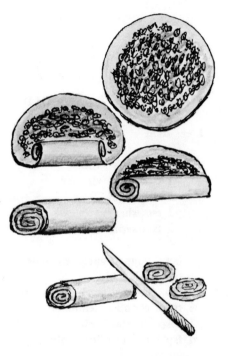

2

Roll the egg skin gently

3

Roll the egg skin gradually

4

Seal the edges with a little beaten egg. Press the edges firmly together

5

After steaming cut the rolls into 1-inch sections

6. Put the rolls on a heatproof platter. Steam in a regular steamer or a big pot (see chapter 1). Pour water in the steamer or pot over high heat. When the water boils, put the platter of rolls into it. Turn to medium heat. Cover and cook about 15-20 minutes or until done. Cut the rolls into 1-inch sections diagonally. (Save the juice for later use.)

7. Heat the remaining oil over a big pan. When the oil is hot, put the celery cabbage into it. Stir-fry about ½ minute. Pour in ingredients (b) and the juice left from the rolls. Stir quickly. Cover and cook about 4-5 minutes or until tender. Then transfer the cabbage to a deep serving dish. Put the egg dumpling on top and *serve hot*.

NOTE: 1. You can cook the egg dumplings ahead and store in the refrigerator a few days. Before serving, cook the celery cabbage as described. After the cabbage is done, transfer the cabbage to a casserole dish and put egg dumplings on top. Cover and heat in a warm oven about 20 minutes and serve hot.
   2. You can serve the whole rolls cold.

10

VEGETABLES

凉拌茄子

COLD EGGPLANT

1 eggplant

(a) 3 tbsp. soy sauce
   1 tsp. white vinegar
   2 tsp. sugar
   1 tsp. sherry
   2 tsp. sesame oil

½ tsp. chopped garlic clove or ¼
   tsp. garlic chips
1 tsp. chopped fresh ginger root
1½ tbsp. chopped scallions
1 tbsp. vegetable oil
½ tsp. monosodium glutamate
   (optional)

1. Boil water in a regular steamer over medium high heat. When the water boils, place the eggplant on top of the steamer. Cover and steam about 25-35 minutes. When the core of the eggplant is tender, remove and let cool.

2. At the same time, heat 1 tbsp. oil in a frying pan over medium heat. Add garlic and ginger. Stir-fry about 5-10 seconds. Then add ingredients (a) and stir quickly. When it boils, remove and add the scallions and monosodium glutamate. Mix well. Let cool.

3. Cut the eggplant into half crosswise. Remove the seeds. Then cut into quarters. Cut each quarter into wedges lengthwise (with the skin on). Arrange on a deep plate in a circular shape . Pour the sauce over it and let stand in the refrigerator for awhile. Serve cold.

NOTE: Be sure each wedge of eggplant is saturated with the sauce.

炸豆腐

FRIED BEAN CURD

4 pieces of square bean curd

(a) mix well:
- ¾ tsp. salt
- ½ tsp. black pepper

(b)
- 1 cup chicken broth
- 2 tsp. Szechuan hot sauce or any substitute hot sauce
- ¼ tsp. salt or salt to taste
- 1 tsp. monosodium glutamate (optional)

(c)
- 1 tbsp. cornstarch
- 1 tbsp. water

¼ cup vegetable oil

1. Cut each bean curd diagonally into two triangular pieces. Then cut each triangular piece parallel to its face into two equal pieces so the total triangular pieces will be sixteen.

2. Dry each bean curd with paper towels. Pour ingredients (a) into a salt shaker. With the salt shaker, sprinkle the mixture on both sides of each triangular bean curd. Let stand for about 5-10 minutes.

3. Heat the oil in a frying pan over medium high heat. When the oil is hot, fry both sides of each bean curd until its color turns brown. Drain on paper towels. Set aside.

4. Leave about two tablespoons of oil in the frying pan over medium high heat. When the oil is hot, add the bean curd and then ingredients (b) over the bean curd. When the sauce boils, turn to medium heat. Cover and cook about 5-6 minutes. Turn each bean curd over at least once during the cooking time. Add the paste ingredients (c). Stir thoroughly. Serve hot or cold.

NOTES: 1. The bean curd can be fried a couple of weeks ahead and stored in the refrigerator. When the bean curd is refrigerated, the cooking time should take longer—about 15-20 minutes over medium heat after the sauce boils.
2. Fresh red or green long hot pepper can be chopped and substituted for the hot sauce.
3. For a spicier taste, add more hot sauce.

鶏油菜心

CELERY CABBAGE IN
CHICKEN SAUCE

2 lb. celery cabbage
1 qt. of water

(a) ½ cup chicken stock
1 tsp. salt

6-8 dried Chinese mushrooms
1 large bamboo shoot (in can)
2 oz. cooked ham (Smithfield preferred)
2 tbsp. vegetable or corn oil
3 tbsp. chicken fat

(b) ½ tsp. salt
1 tsp. sugar
1 tsp. monosodium glutamate (optional)
½ cup chicken stock

(c) 2 tbsp. cornstarch
2 tbsp. water

1. Discard tough outer leaves of the cabbage. Trim off a small piece of the bottom of the cabbage. Then separate the leaves of the cabbage. Wash leaves and drain well. Also, separate the stalk and the tender part of each leaf. Split stalks lengthwise in half. Cut them crosswise into 2 or 3-inch sections. Cut the tender parts into halves if too long.

2. Place the mushrooms in a mixing bowl. Add boiling water to cover about 15-20 minutes. Drain and squeeze to remove excess moisture. Cut off and discard the tough stems. Cut the caps into quarters.

3. Wash the bamboo shoots. Cut into tree-shaped slices.

4. Chop the cooked ham into small dices and set aside.

5. Boil 6-8 cups of water in a big pot over medium high heat. Add the stalk parts of the cabbage. Stir and cover. Cook about 4-5 minutes until crispy and tender. Drain and rinse under cold running water. Then drain well and set aside. (This part can be done well ahead of time.)

6. Heat 2 tbsp. oil in a big frying pan over medium high heat. When the oil is hot, place the tender part of the cabbage leaves into the pan. Stir quickly and add 4 tbsp. water. Stir-fry about 1-2 minutes. Add the stalk parts, mushrooms, bamboo shoots, and ingredients (a). Stir-fry together. Cover and cook about ½-1 minute until heated through. Remove the cabbage to a deep serving plate with a slotted spoon. Drain the liquid away from the pan. Keep the cabbage in the oven or on a hot plate.

7. Heat 3 tbsp. chicken fat in the pan over medium heat. Add ingredients (b). Stir well. Blend ingredients (c) into a paste and add to the pan gradually while stirring the sauce. Stir until transparent and thickened. Pour over the cabbage. Garnish with diced ham. Serve immediately.

炒白菜

C: 6-8 Servings
W: 4-5 Servings

STIR-FRY CHINESE CABBAGE
(BOK CHOY)

2 lbs. Chinese cabbage
¾ tsp. salt or salt to taste
½ cup chicken broth
3 tbsp. vegetable oil
1 tsp. monosodium glutamate
(optional)

1. Wash and clean the cabbage thoroughly. Cut each leaf lengthwise into half and cut each half crosswise into 1½-inch sections. Peel the skin of the main stem in the center if it is too big. Cut it into 1½-inch slices. Separate the white stems and green leaves.

2. Pour 3 tbsp. oil into the frying pan over medium high heat. When the oil is hot, add the white stems. Stir about 1 minute. Add the salt and chicken broth. Stir and cover. Cook a couple of minutes. Then add the leaves and stir quickly. Add monosodium glutamate and stir. Cook about 1 minute or until tender, but still crunchy. Place in the serving plate and serve hot.

NOTE: Quartered dried Chinese mushrooms may be added to the cabbage, if desired. Soak the mushrooms in boiling water 15-20 minutes, then drain and squeeze out excess moisture. Cut off and discard the tough stems.

129

炒布羅可里菜

STIR-FRY BROCCOLI CUP

1 lb. broccoli cup (the entire broccoli)
½ tsp. salt or salt to taste
3 tbsp. sugar
¼ tsp. monosodium glutamate (optional)
2 tbsp. chicken broth
2 tbsp. vegetable oil

1. Discard any brown leaves. Pinch the good broccoli into 2-inch long sections. Peel off the skin of the hard stems and cut stems into strips.

2. Heat 2 tbsp. oil in the frying pan over medium high heat. Sprinkle ½ tsp. salt over the pan. When the oil is hot, add the broccoli. Stir quickly and pour 2 tbsp. chicken broth into the pan. Cover and cook about ½-1 minute. If it is not salty enough, salt to taste. Uncover and stir continuously. Add sugar and monosodium glutamate. Stir about ½ minute or until tender, but still crunchy. Serve hot or cold.

炒蒲公英

STIR-FRY DANDELION

1 lb. dandelion
½ tsp. salt or to taste
1 tbsp. chicken broth or water
2½ tbsp. sugar
1 tsp. monosodium glutamate (optional)
2 tbsp. vegetable oil

1. Wash dandelion very well. Pinch off the top roots, the buds, and the yellow spoiled parts, if any. Cut into 3-inch long sections.

2. Heat oil in the frying pan over medium high heat. When the oil is hot, add the dandelion and stir quickly. Add salt and chicken broth or water. Stir constantly about 1 minute. Add sugar and monosodium glutamate and stir about ½ minute more. Serve hot.

COLD CUCUMBERS

2 **cucumbers**
1 **oz. agar agar (optional)**
¼ **lb. boiled ham**
1 **egg**

(a) 2 **tbsp. sugar**
1 **tsp. white vinegar**
1¼ **tsp. salt**
1 **tsp. monosodium gluta-**
mate (optional)
1 **tbsp. sesame oil**

2 **tbsp. vegetable or corn oil**

1. Peel the cucumbers and trim off the ends and discard. Cut the cucumbers in half lengthwise and scoop out the seeds with a spoon. Divide the cucumber into 3 or 4 sections crosswise depending upon the length of the cucumber. Then cut each section lengthwise into shreds. Place in a bowl and set in the refrigerator.

2. Hold and rinse the agar agar under the cold running water for a couple of minutes. Then the agar agar will be clean and soft. Cut into sections the same size as the cucumbers.

3. Cut the boiled ham into shreds about 2 inches long.

4. Beat the egg well with ⅛ tsp. salt. Heat 1 tbsp. oil in the pan over medium heat. Swirl the pan so the oil covers the bottom of the pan. When the oil is hot, pour half of the beaten egg into the pan and swing the pan around quickly so the egg will cover the pan. When the egg becomes firm, use a spatula to transfer the thin egg disc to a plate. Pour the remaining 1 tbsp. oil to the pan. Repeat the procedure to get another egg cake. Cut the egg cakes into 2-inch long shreds. Set aside.

5. One hour before serving, mix the cucumber and agar agar well and then add ingredients (a). Mix them very well. Garnish with boiled ham and egg shreds. Put in the refrigerator until ready to serve.

凉拌龍鬚菜
COLD ASPARAGUS

2 lbs. asparagus
6 cups boiling water

(a)   3 tbsp. soy sauce
     2 tsp. sugar
  1-1½ tbsp. sesame oil or salad oil
     ¼ tsp. monosodium gluta-
        mate (optional)
     ¼ tsp. salt or to taste

1. Wash the asparagus thoroughly. Break off the tough part of the asparagus (near the roots) and discard. Cut the tender parts of the asparagus into long, rolling-knife pieces (see chapter 1).

2. Place the asparagus in 6 cups of boiling water. Heat until water boils again. Let it boil about 1-2 minutes (until it is crispy), depending on the size of the asparagus. Then drain and chill under cold running water. Store in the refrigerator until the asparagus is well chilled and marinated.

3. At least ½ hour (not more than 2 hours) before serving, mix the asparagus with ingredients (a). Salt to taste. Store again in the refrigerator until serving time.

凉拌波菜和五香豆腐干

SPINACH WITH SPICED BEAN
CURD CAKE

1 lb. spinach
2 squares of spiced soy bean cake
1 qt. water

(a)   2 tbsp. sesame oil
     ¼ tsp. salt or salt to taste
     ½ tsp. monosodium gluta-
        mate (optional)
     1 tsp. sugar

1. Wash and clean the spinach. Drain well. Boil 1 qt. of water in a big pot over medium high heat. When the water boils, add the spinach and remove the pot from the heat. Let the spinach soak about ½-1 minute; then drain and rinse under cold running water. Drain well, squeezing off the excess water from the spinach. Chop into very small pieces.

2. Chop the two squares of bean cakes into very small dices.

3. Mix the chopped spinach and diced bean curd together with ingredients (a). Mix very well. Taste; if not salty enough, salt to taste. Serve cold.

蕃茄燒豆腐

C: 4-6 Servings
W: 2-3 Servings

TOMATOES WITH BEAN CURD

8 oz. tomatoes
3 squares of bean curd
3 tbsp. vegetable oil

(a)   **2 tbsp. soy sauce**
    ½ tsp. salt or salt to taste
    1 tsp. sugar
    ½ tsp. monosodium gluta-
    mate (optional)

1. Parboil tomatoes about 2 minutes. Peel off the skin and scoop out and discard the seeds. Cut into thick slices.

2. Wash the bean curds and cut into halves. Then cut into about 1″ x ½″ slices.

3. Heat 3 tbsp. oil in a frying pan over medium high heat. When the oil is hot, add the tomatoes. Fry about 1 or 2 minutes. Add the bean curds and fry a few minutes. Add ingredients (a) and stir-fry for a while until the mixture bubbles again. Serve hot.

133

肉皮炒白菜

FRIED PORK RINDS WITH
CELERY CABBAGE

1 lb. celery cabbage
½ tsp. salt

(a) ⅓ bag of Fried Pork Rinds
     (e.g. Filler's Bacon Crisp,
     2⅜ oz. bag), soaked in ¼
     cup of water
     ¼ tsp. salt
     2 tbsp. chicken broth or
     stock

(b) ½ tsp. cornstarch
     1 tbsp. water
     ½ tsp. monosodium gluta-
     mate (optional)

1. Wash the celery cabbage clean. Cut lengthwise into halves. Then cut crosswise into 2-inch sections. Keep the white stem parts and green leaves separate.

2. Soak ⅓ bag of the Fried Pork Rinds with ¼ cup of water for a few minutes.

3. Heat 2 tbsp. oil in a big frying pan over medium high heat. Sprinkle ½ tsp. salt over the oil. When the oil is hot (bubbles), put the white stem parts of the cabbage into the pan. Stir constantly about 1-2 minutes. Then add the leaves and ingredients (a). Stir well and cover to cook about 1-2 minutes. Take off the cover and stir until tender (taste one white stem). Add the paste ingredients (b), and stir well until it thickens. Serve hot.

NOTE: 1. Chinese cabbage may substitute for the celery cabbage.
      2. Dried bean curd may substitute for Fried Pork Rinds; see Instruction 5 on Vegetables, chapter 2.

DRY COOKED STRING BEANS

1 lb. string beans

(a) 2 tbsp. dry shrimp
   1½ oz. Szechuan preserved
       cabbage
   2 tsp. chopped ginger root

(b) 1 tbsp. soy sauce
    1 tbsp. sugar
    1 tsp. white vinegar
    1 tsp. salt or salt to taste
    2 tbsp. chicken broth
    ½ tsp. monosodium gluta-
        mate (optional)

1 tbsp. sesame oil
2 tbsp. chopped scallions
4 cups vegetable oil

1. Wash and dry the string beans thoroughly. Remove the tips of the beans
   and cut in half if too long.

2. Soak the dry shrimp in warm water about 15 minutes. Chop them into
   small pieces. Chop the Szechuan preserved cabbage into small pieces.

3. Pour oil into a deep pot over medium high heat. When the oil is hot, add
   the beans. Stir-fry until the beans shrink and wrinkle, about 3-4 minutes.
   Remove the beans from the oil. Let the oil cool in the deep pot.

4. Use another frying pan with 2 tbsp. oil over medium high heat. When the
   oil is hot, add ingredients (a). Stir quickly for a few seconds. Return the
   beans and stir continuously. Then add ingredients (b) and stir very well,
   about ½ minute. Add the sesame oil and stir thoroughly. Place the beans
   on the serving plate. Serve hot.

NOTE: This dish can be kept in the refrigerator for a few days and can also be
       served cold.

135

辣白菜

CABBAGE WITH DRIED
RED PEPPERS

1½-2 lb. cabbage
6 tbsp. vegetable oil

(a) 15 small dried red peppers
½ tbsp. chopped ginger root
or ½ tsp. ginger powder

(b) 1 tbsp. soy sauce
1 tsp. sherry
1 tbsp. sugar
½ tbsp. vinegar
½ tbsp. sesame oil
½ tsp. monosodium gluta-
mate (optional)

1 tsp. salt or salt to taste

1. Wash the cabbage and cut into 2-inch wide pieces. Set aside.

2. Wash the dried red peppers. Cut off the ends and discard the seeds. Chop into 1-inch sections if longer than 1 inch.

3. Heat 5 tbsp. oil in a frying pan over medium high heat. When the oil is piping hot add the cabbage. Stir-fry with 1 tsp. salt until the cabbage is barely soft, about 1 minute. If it is not salty enough, salt to taste. Remove the cabbage and leave the oil in the pan.

4. Add an additional 1 tbsp. oil to that remaining in the pan over medium high heat. When the oil is hot, stir-fry ingredients (a) for ½ minute. Add the cabbage and ingredients (b). Stir-fry constantly until heated thoroughly. Serve hot or cold.

炒花椰菜

CAULIFLOWER WITH WATER CHESTNUTS

1 medium cauliflower
2 tbsp. oil
5 dried Chinese or fresh mushrooms
6 water chestnuts (from can)

(a) ¾ cup chicken broth
1 tsp. sherry
2 tbsp. soy sauce
1 tsp. oil
½ tsp. monosodium gluta-
mate (optional)
½ tsp. salt or salt to taste

(b) 1 tbsp. cornstarch
2 tbsp. water

1. Break the cauliflower into pieces. Parboil by pouring boiling water over it. Cover and let stand for 5 to 10 minutes. Then drain well and set aside.

2. If you use Chinese dried mushrooms, soak them in boiling water for 15 minutes. Drain and squeeze away the water. Cut the hard part of the stems from the mushroom caps, and cut each cap into quarters.

3. Slice the water chestnuts.

4. Heat 2 tbsp. oil in a frying pan over medium high heat. Saute the mushrooms (if fresh) for a few seconds. Add the water chestnuts and ingredients (a). Stir and simmer a few seconds. Then add the cauliflower. Stir and cover to cook about 3 to 5 minutes. Taste; if not salty enough, salt to taste. Blend ingredients (b) into a paste and add to the pan. Stir constantly until thickened. Serve immediately.

凉拌芥菜

COLD MUSTARD GREENS

1 lb. mustard greens

(a)   **½ tsp. salt**
      3 tbsp. soy sauce
  1½-2 tsp. sugar
    1 tsp. sesame or salad oil
    ¼ tsp. monosodium gluta-
      mate (optional)

1. Separate the leaves of the mustard greens. Wash leaves and drain well. Separate the stalk and the tender part of each leaf. Split stalks lengthwise into half. Then cut them into 1½-inch sections. Cut the tender parts into halves, if too long. Otherwise use as is.

2. There are two ways to cook the mustard greens:
   a. If a strong mustard flavor is desired, heat a deep frying pan over medium high heat. When it is very hot, throw the stem parts into the pan and stir vigorously about 1-2 minutes (try not to let them burn). Then put the leaves in and stir about one more minute. Transfer to a large bowl and immediately cover tightly. Let it stand until cooled. Put in the refrigerator until ready to use.
   b. If a mild mustard flavor is desired, boil water in a big pot over medium high heat. When the water boils, pour over the stem parts and cover about 2-3 minutes. Then put the leaves in and cover tightly until the greens are crispy and cold. Drain the water off and store in the refrigerator until ready to use.

3. One hour before serving, mix ingredients (a) with the mustard greens very well. Salt to taste and store in the refrigerator until ready to serve.

11

DESSERTS
AND PASTRY

拔絲香蕉

CANDIED BANANA FRITTERS

3 bananas
1 egg
6 tbsp. sugar
3 tbsp. flour
2 tsp. fried sesame seeds
3 tbsp. cornstarch
1 tbsp. water

1. Beat egg; add flour, cornstarch and water and beat into a paste.

2. Peel bananas and cut each into 5 diagonal pieces. Coat with egg paste and deep-fry for 15 seconds. Remove the bananas and drain. Keep the oil hot.

3. In another pan, heat 2 tbsp. oil. Add sugar and stir over medium heat until the sugar melts.

4. Deep-fry the bananas a second time in the original pot until golden brown. Remove when the melted sugar in the second pan becomes a syrup, add the bananas and sesame seeds, stirring constantly until the bananas are coated evenly with syrup.

5. Serve the fritters on a plate that has been coated with oil.

NOTE: Fritters should also be served with a bowl of cold water for dipping. This solidifies the sugar and makes eating easier.

EGG ROLLS

For the skin:
- 1 egg
- 2 cups flour
- ½ cup cornstarch
- 1 tsp. salt
- ⅔ cup water
- flour
- (Egg roll skin can be bought in Chinese grocery stores. There are about 14-16 pieces in a 1-lb. package.)

For the filling:
- 1 lb. ground beef (lean boneless beef, ground once)
- ½ lb. shrimp, shelled, deveined and chopped
- 2 slices of ginger root
- ½ cup chopped scallions
- 2 cups shredded celery
- 4 cups shredded cabbage
- 1 tsp. salt
- ½ tsp. garlic powder
- 1½ cups diced water chestnuts (canned or fresh)
- 6 cups vegetable oil

(a)
- 1 tsp. sherry
- ½ tsp. cornstarch
- ½ tsp. sugar
- 1½ tsp. salt or salt to taste
- dash of pepper

(b)
- ¼ tsp. salt
- ½ tsp. sherry
- ½ tsp. cornstarch

(c)
- 1 tsp. monosodium glutamate (optional)
- 1 tbsp. cornstarch

(d) for the paste:
- 1 egg white
- 2 tbsp. water

140

THE SKIN:

1. Beat the egg, then combine with flour, cornstarch, salt, and water. Knead until smooth and elastic, about 5 minutes. If it is too hard, wet your hands and knead again. Cover with a damp cloth and refrigerate ½-1 hour.

2. Sprinkle some flour on a board. Place the dough on it. Shape into a 12-inch long roll. Cut into 4 equal sections. Roll each section into 4-inch long pieces and then into 4 inch-long portions. With a rolling pin, roll each portion into a 6½ or 7-inch square. About 16 square egg roll skins will be obtained. Keep the skins covered with a cloth as you work. After you finish (before stacking them), rub each skin with flour to prevent them from sticking to each other. Wrap the skins and store in the refrigerator until ready to use.

THE FILLING:

1. Mix the ground beef with ingredients (a) and mix the shrimp with ingredients (b). Let stand about ½ hour.

2. Heat 3 tbsp. oil in a big frying pan over medium high heat. When the oil is hot, add one ginger slice and stir well. Then add the ground beef. Stir-fry quickly and separate the ground beef into loose pieces. Remove and set aside.

2. Using the same frying pan with 2 tbsp. oil, add another piece of ginger. When the oil is hot, add the shrimp and stir very fast for about ½ minute. Remove and set aside.

4. Drain the ground beef oil and shrimp oil into a frying pan. When it is hot, add the cabbage and celery. Cook for about ½ minute. Add 1 tsp. salt, scallions, and garlic powder and stir about ½ minute. Return the ground beef and shrimp to the pan and mix well. Stir about another 10-20 seconds or until done. If it is not salty enough, salt to taste.

5. Drain the filling over a colander until amost dry (about two hours). Transfer the filling to a large bowl. Add the diced water chestnuts and ingredients (c). Mix very well.

6. Blend ingredients (d) to a sticky solution as a paste for wrapping the rolls.

EGG ROLLS:

(1)

Place 2 tbsp. of filling on an egg roll skin at the corner near you.

(2)

Fold the corner of the skin near you over the filling until it is just covered.

(3)

Brush the left edges and corner of the triangle with the egg paste. Fold over to the center.

(4)

Brush the right edges and corner of the triangle with egg paste. Fold over to the center. Press down to seal, making a kind of envelope.

(5)

Brush the remaining edges and the last corner with paste. Roll the enclosed filling into a cylinder.

(6)

Finish by rolling the enclosed filling in the rest of the skin. Seal it firmly.

1. Place 2-3 tbsp. of filling on an egg roll skin at the corner near you (see illustration). Fold the corner of the skin pointing at you over the filling until it is just covered. Brush the right and left corners of the triangles with the egg paste. Fold over the corners. Press down firmly to seal, making a kind of envelope. Brush the flap of the envelope with the egg paste and roll one more turn into a cylinder and seal firmly with the furthest corner. Set aside until the egg roll skins are used up. If there is some filling left, you can eat it as an ordinary dish, or save it for more egg roll skins.

2. Heat the oil in a deep frying pan or deep fryer (about 350° F). Fry the egg rolls until golden brown (about 10-15 minutes) and crispy. Drain on paper towels. Serve plain or with sweet plum or mustard sauce. Serve immediately and hot.

NOTE: 1. If you do not have a deep fryer with a temperature gauge, just drop a little piece of bread into the oil. When there are bubbles, the oil is ready.

2. If you want to freeze the egg rolls for later use, just deep fry for about 5 minutes or until light brown. Before serving, deep fry another 5-10 minutes.

3. The egg rolls can be kept in the oven until ready to serve.

杏仁豆腐   *4-6 Servings*

JELLED ALMOND FRUIT DESSERT

1 bag Knox unflavored gelatin
1 cup boiling water, less one tablespoon
1 tbsp. cold water
1 cup milk
1 can mandarin orange segments or 1 can lichee fruit
3 tbsp. sugar
1 tsp. almond extract

1. Dissolve gelatin with 1 tbsp. cold water. Mix well in a measuring cup. Add boiling water to the measuring cup until one cup.

2. Pour 3 tbsp. of sugar into a deep square or rectangular container. Pour the hot mixture of gelatin over the sugar and stir until all the sugar is dissolved. Then add 1 cup milk and 1 tsp. almond extract to the container. Mix well and store in the refrigerator for several hours, until firm.

3. Before serving, cut the almond gelatin into 1-inch cubes. Mix with mandarin orange or lichee segments. Serve cold.

STEAMED ROLLS AND
FANCY ROLLS

3 cups flour
1 cup lukewarm water
1 tsp. sugar
1 package or cake of dry or com-
pressed active yeast
1 tsp. salt
2 tsp. sesame oil or vegetable oil

1. Mix the yeast, sugar and lukewarm water very well and let stand for 4 or 5 minutes until the yeast bubbles up.

2. Pour the mixture slowly into the flour with your left hand while you are mixing the flour with your right fingers. If it is still dry, add 1 or 1½ tbsp. warm water. Knead it by pushing down, pushing it forward, then turning it back on itself. Repeat the kneading process for 5 or 6 minutes until the dough is soft and smooth. Place the dough in a bowl which should be big enough to allow the dough to grow to four times its original size. Cover with a dampened cloth. Let stand in a warm place (70° F or more) for about 1 or 2 hours. In the winter, put the dough in a slightly warmed oven. It will rise 3 or 4 times bigger than the original dough, with a lot of holes inside. When risen, take out and knead down again. Divide dough into halves and roll each half into a flat piece (about 15 inches across). Use about 2 tbsp. dusting flour to prevent sticking during rolling.

3. Brush 1 tsp. vegetable oil on the surface of each piece and sprinkle ½ tsp. salt evenly over the surface of each piece. Roll it up like a carpet before dancing. This operation will slightly lengthen the dough, so that the resulting long roll will now be about 18 inches. Cut each piece of dough into 8 equal sections. Cover with a dampened cloth. Press one-third the way down on the middle of each section with broad back of a chopping knife parallel with the original cutting. The result is a Fancy Roll dough. Repeat with all 16 sections.

4. Cover with a dampened towel. Put on a flat plate and set aside for 20-30 minutes. When you press the skin of the roll, it should bounce back right away. This is the time to put the skins into a steamer or use a steamer substitute (described in chapter 1). Heat the water to boiling over medium high heat. Line the top section of the steamer with a dampened cheesecloth; then place the rolls on the cheesecloth or place the rolls in a plate. Put the first plate of rolls in the steamer or on a rack. Cover the pan tightly. Steam over medium high heat about 10-15 minutes. Watch the

water in the steamer. Replenish with boiling water if evaporated. If you are doing more than one batch, return the first batch of rolls to the steamer after the second batch is done, piling them on the rolls still in the steamer. Reheat 3 or 4 minutes.

NOTE: The rolls can be put in plastic bags for the refrigerator or stored in the freezer.

杏仁餅

40 cookies

CHINESE ALMOND COOKIES

(a) 2½ cups flour
1 tsp. baking powder
2 tsp. baking soda
1½ cups sugar

1 cup lard

(b) 1 tsp. almond extract
1 egg
¼ tsp. salt
1 tbsp. water (more if necessary but do not make too soft a dough.)
whole natural almonds

1. Stir ingredients (a) together in a bowl.

2. Cut lard and sugar into the mixture of ingredients (a) with knife or pastry blender until fluffy. Add ingredients (b). With your fingers, knead thoroughly to make dough pliable. Let it stand 5 minutes in a cool place.

3. Form dough into balls 1½" in diameter (about the size of a walnut). Press with palm to flatten to ½" thick. Press an almond in the center. Repeat this step until all the dough is used.

4. Preheat oven to 375°F. Bake the cookies at 375°F for 7 minutes; then reduce to 325°F and bake for 7-8 minutes or until cookies are light golden brown.

NOTE: Due to the differences in ovens, the temperature can vary. Watch the cookies carefully in order to judge the cooking time in your oven.

八寶粥

EIGHT JEWEL CONGEE

2 tbsp. tapioca
(a)   **2 tbsp. aduki beans (red**
        beans)
      2 tbsp. mung beans (green
        beans)
      2 tbsp. peanuts
      2 tbsp. lotus seeds
      2 tbsp. gingko nuts
      2 tbsp. glutinous rice
      2 tbsp. barley
12 red dates
1 cup sugar
10 cups water

1. Wash red dates and cook them in 1½ cups water over medium high heat. After the water boils, turn to low heat about 1 hour or until their skins soften. Set aside.

2. Soak tapioca in the cold water for at least 6-8 hours.

3. Wash and drain ingredients (a) well. Place in a deep pot with 4 cups of water over medium high heat. When the water boils, turn to very low heat (*warm* on an electric range). Cook about 1½-2 hours or until the ingredients are tender and soft. Stir occasionally to prevent the ingredients from sticking to the bottom. (You may use a pressure cooker; it will take about ½ hour.)

4. After cooking ingredients (a) for ½ hour, heat 1½ cups water in another pot over medium high heat. When the water boils, drain the soaked tapioca and pour into it. Stir and turn to very low heat. Cook about ¾-1 hour until the tapioca becomes transparent.

5. Pour the tapioca into the large pot with ingredients (a). Add 1½ cups water. Stir and cook over low heat. When it boils, add sugar. Stir well.

6. Pour the congee into serving bowls. Garnish with red dates. Serve hot.

NOTE: 1. If you use small bowls, you can get 8-9 servings.
       2. Congee can be cooked ahead and put in the refrigerator. Reheat and serve. (The addition of some more water may be necessary.)

饅頭

STEAMED BUNS (MAN-TOU)

3 cups flour
½ cup warm water
2 tbsp. sugar
1 package or cake of dry or
compressed active yeast
½ cup lukewarm milk

1. Mix the yeast and sugar with lukewarm water and milk very well. Let it stand for 4 or 5 minutes until the yeast bubbles up.

2. Pour the mixture slowly into the flour with your left hand while you are mixing the flour with your right fingers. If it is still dry, add 1 or 1½ tbsp. warm water. Knead it by pressing down, pushing it forward, then turning it back on itself. Repeat the kneading process for 5 or 6 minutes until the dough is soft and smooth. Place the dough in a bowl which should be big enough to allow the dough to grow to 4 times its original size. Cover with a dampened cloth. Let stand in a warm place (70° F or more) for about 1½ or 2 hours. (If in warm weather, only 1½ or 2 hours are needed. If in cold temperature, 3 or 4 hours may be necessary.) The dough will rise about 4 times bigger than the original dough with a lot of holes inside.

3. Take the dough out and knead it down again, using some dusting flour to keep it from sticking to your fingers. Roll the dough into a uniform bar, cut into 16 equal portions. With your thumbs and index fingers, work each portion with a sort of wrapping and tucking motion from outside in, so as to bring out a dome and a bottom, like a hot roll.

4. Put on a flat plate and cover with a dry towel. Set aside for 20-30 minutes for a second rising. When you push its skin down, it should bounce back again. Then line the top section of the steamer with a dampened cheese-cloth. Steam the buns in a steamer over medium high heat or in a steamer substitute (described in chapter 1). When the water boils, cover tightly and steam about 10-15 minutes. If you have two batches, return the first batch to the steamer after the second batch is done. Reheat 3 or 4 minutes and serve hot.

NOTE: 1. Understeaming or oversteaming and underrising or overrising may cause dark unrisen spots.
2. You can do the buns ahead and store in the refrigerator until needed. Then steam and serve hot.

煮餃子

BOILED DUMPLINGS (JAO-TZE)

For the skin:
  4 cups flour
  1½-2 cups cold water

For the filling:
12 oz. ground pork
(a)   3 cups chopped celery cabbage
     4½ tbsp. soy sauce
     ½ tsp. ginger root, chopped fine
     ¾ tsp. salt or salt to taste
     ½ tsp. sesame oil or 2 tsp. vegetable oil
     1½ tbsp. cornstarch
     ½ tsp. monosodium glutamate (optional)
     ¼ cup scallion, chopped fine
     1 tbsp. sherry

For dip:
(b)   2 tbsp. vinegar
     ¼ cup soy sauce

1. For the skin, place the flour in a big bowl. Pour the water gradually while mixing with your fingers. Knead evenly about 5 minutes using dusting flour on the kneading board to prevent sticking. Cover the dough with a damp cloth and let it stand for at least ½ hour. Divide it into 4 parts. Cut the dough into bars of about equal thickness. Use a measuring stick to measure the bars. Then cut the total length into 15 equal parts according to the measuring stick, place in a clean bowl and cover with a damp cloth. Work each piece with your fingers into a circular shape. Then roll it flat with a rolling pin to about 3½ inches in diameter and about ⅛ inch thick, rolling it thinner around the edges than the center.

2. For the filling, mix the pork and ingredients (a) very well. Let stand at least ½ hour.

3. Place 1-2 tbsp. of the meat filling in the center of the circular skin. Wrap the circle of the skin around the meat filling as illustrated. Make six folds on ⅔ of the circle so that it puckers up into a hollow on one side. Fold the straight ⅓ of the skin over the puckered half and pinch to seal the skin all along the edges as illustrated. Then the dumpling is ready to cook.

148

(1)

Place 2 tbsp. of the meat filling in the center of the circular skin.

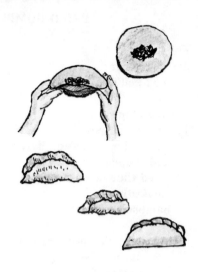

(2)

Wrap the circle of the skin around the meat filling.

(3)

Make six folds on ⅔ of the circle so that it puckers up into a hollow on one side. Fold the straight ⅓ of the skin over the puckered half and pinch to seal.

4. Bring about 4-5 quarts of water to a vigorous boil over medium high heat. Add the dumplings gently and quickly one at a time. This will stop the boiling for a while. After boiling starts again, pour in 2 cups of water and turn to medium heat. After the third boiling, pour in 2 more cups of water. After the third addition of water, the dumplings are ready to serve.

5. Remove the dumplings with a slotted spoon. The starchy soup can be served, if desired. Serve the dumplings with ingredients (b) as a dip. Vinegar, soy sauce or a combination of both can also be used as a sauce.

NOTE: 1. Boiled dumplings can be fried. Place the boiled dumplings on a lightly greased platter to cool. Heat ¼ inch of oil in one or two frying pans over medium heat. When the oil is hot, put the dumplings bottom side down in the oil. Cover and cook until brown. Turn and cook on another side until brown. Serve with vinegar or dumpling sauce.

2. Dumpling sauce:
   4 tbsp. soy sauce
   1 tbsp. minced ginger root
   1 tsp. minced garlic
   1 tbsp. chopped scallion
   1 tsp. sugar
   ½ tsp. monosodium glutamate (optional)
   ¼ tsp. white vinegar (optional)
   ¼ tsp. sesame oil (if obtainable)
   Stir the ingredients in a mixing bowl. Blend well and serve with fried dumplings.

炸餃子(鍋貼)

FRIED DUMPLINGS (KUO-TIEH)

For the skin:
2½ cups flour
⅔ cup boiling water

For the filling:
10 oz. ground pork
 6 oz. shrimp, shelled, deveined
   and chopped
 5 dried Chinese mushrooms
   (soaked)
 2 bamboo shoots

(a) 1 tbsp. chopped scallions
   ½ tsp. minced ginger root (if
     obtainable)
   2 tbsp. soy sauce
   ½ tsp. salt or salt to taste
  1½ tsp. cornstarch
   2 tbsp. chicken broth
   ½ tsp. sugar

 2 cups chopped celery cabbage
   (optional)
¼ cup vegetable oil or corn oil
¾ cup water

1. Place the flour in a large bowl. Add boiling water gradually and mix well with a wooden spoon or chopstick. Add some drops of cold water. Knead dough with fingers until thoroughly mixed. Cover with a damp cloth and let stand for at least ½ hour.

2. Meanwhile, squeeze the soaked mushrooms and chop into fine pieces. Also chop the bamboo shoots. Mix the pork, shrimp, mushrooms, bamboo shoots, celery and ingredients (a) very well. Let stand for ½ hour.

3. Knead the dough on lightly floured pastry board. Roll it with palms and fingers into sausage shape. Cut the sausage into half. Keep ½ covered with a damp cloth. Shape the other half into evenly thick sausage shape. Use a measuring stick to measure and then cut into equal 18 pieces. Cover with a damp cloth. With the same method cut the other half into 18 pieces too. Also cover with a damp cloth. Then, with the palm, roll each piece into a ball and flatten into a cake shape. Using a floured rolling pin, roll each cake into 3 or 3½-inch circle ⅛ inch thick. Roll the edges thinner than the center.

芙

蓉

蛋

Egg Foo Yung (p. 122)

中國烹飪

中國烹飪

熊余文琴著

凉拌龍鬚菜

Cold Asparagus (p. 132)

中國烹飪

中國烹飪

熊余文琴著

4. Fill the center of each circular piece with about 1-2 tbsp. of the pork mixture as you do for the boiled dumplings (see index). As each dumpling is finished, place it on a lightly floured board. Cover with a cloth to prevent drying out. Repeat the same process until all the dumplings are made.

5. Heat 2 tbsp. oil in a big flat-lidded frying pan. When it is hot, add the dumplings, bottom side down. Cook about 2 minutes or until golden brown. Pour ¾ cup water all around the dumplings and cover as tightly as possible with the lid. Cook over medium high heat until the water has almost boiled away (about 5 minutes). Add 1 tbsp. oil to the side of the pan and fry another ½ minute. Remove from the heat and place a serving plate over the frying pan and invert the pan quickly. Put in a warm oven. Now prepare the remaining portions until all dumplings are fried. Serve with dumpling sauce (See index) or vinegar.

肉包子，甜包子   *16 Buns*

STEAMED STUFFED BUNS

For the skin:
See recipe for steamed buns. After the first rising, divide the dough into 24 parts and roll them with rolling pin into 3½-4-inch diameter discs. If you want to make larger buns you can divide the dough into 20 parts and roll them into 4- or 5- inch diameter discs. Cover and set aside.

For the filling:
 I. **Meat filling**
     1 lb. ground pork
     1 lb. celery cabbage or water-
     cress

(a)   **2 tbsp. soy sauce**
      1 tsp. sugar
      2 scallions, chopped
      1 tsp. salt, or salt to taste
      ¼ tsp. fresh ginger root or
      ginger powder
      1 tbsp. sesame oil
      1 tbsp. cornstarch

151

1. Buy a lean boneless pork butt. Ask the butcher to grind the meat once (only once) for you.

2. Wash the cabbage and chop it very fine. Squeeze most of its liquid off by straining hard in a dry cloth.

3. Mix thoroughly the ground pork, the chopped cabbage and ingredients (a). Set aside.

II. Sweet filling

(b)   2 oz. pecans, ground fine
      2 oz. walnuts, ground fine
      2 oz. almonds, ground fine
      2 oz. sesame seeds, roasted
        in frying pan over medium
        heat about 1 or 2 minutes
      1 cup sugar
    6-8 tbsp. lard (melted)

1. Mix ingredients (b) very well as sweet filling, if you want to make sweet buns.

To make the buns:

1. Place one of the prepared discs of dough in the palm of your hand and put about 1 or 2 tsp. (for small buns) of the filling in the center of the dough. With your fingers, turn up the rim bit by bit to wrap around the filling until only a small opening is left at top center. Close the top by pinching the edges together. This is the steamed meat-filled bun. For sweet fillings, after closing the dough around the filling roll the bun between the palms of your hands to turn it into a smooth ball. Repeat until all the discs are filled.

2. Put aside again for 20-30 minutes for a second rising. When ready, the skin will bounce back again when pressed. Cut 20 pieces of 2-inch square wax-paper. Place one piece of wax-paper on the bottom of each of the buns. Then steam them in a regular steamer or in a steamer substitute described in chapter 1, about 10-20 minutes over medium high heat. Put on a heated platter. If you have two batches, return the first batch to the steamer when the second batch is done, and steam about 3 or 4 minutes. Serve hot.

NOTE: 1. You may substitute pork with roast pork, shrimp, crabmeat or chicken. Also you may substitute celery cabbage with spinach, leeks, or watercress.

2. The steamed stuffed buns can be stored and frozen in plastic bags.

3. You can use ready-made hot roll mix as the skin. Prepare according to the directions on the box of hot roll mix (omitting the addition of eggs). After the dough rises, divide into 24 parts. Roll each part into a 3-inch diameter disc, using the same method as above.

(1)

Put about 1 or 2 tbsp. of the filling in the center of the dough disc.

(2)

With your fingers turn up the rim bit by bit to wrap around the filling until only a small opening is left at top center.

(3)

Close the top by pinching the edges together.

(4)

Set the bun aside with its twisted side up. This is a steamed bun with meat filling.

(5)

Roll the bun between the palms of your hands to turn into a smooth ball. This is a steamed bun with sweet filling.

豬肉絲春捲

20 Spring rolls

SPRING ROLLS

For the skin:
Buy the skin from a Chinese grocery store or make egg roll skin (see index) (20 spring roll skins).

For the filling:
1 lb. shredded pork
½ lb. shrimp, shelled, deveined and chopped
6 shredded scallions

(a) 3 tbsp. soy sauce
1 tbsp. cornstarch

(b) ½ tsp. salt
½ tsp. sherry
1 tsp. cornstarch

1 lb. bean sprouts
½ lb. celery cabbage

(c) 1 tbsp. soy sauce
1 tsp. salt
1 tsp. sugar

(d) 1 tbsp. cornstarch
½ tsp. monosodium glutamate (optional)
½ small can water chestnuts, shredded (optional)

For paste:

(e) 1 egg white
2 tbsp. water

1. Marinate the shredded pork with ingredients (a) and marinate the shrimp with ingredients (b). Let stand about ½ hour.

2. Shred the celery cabbage into 1½-inch long strips. Wash and discard the brown tails of the bean sprouts and drain well.

154

3. Heat 4 tbsp. oil in the frying pan over medium high heat. Add the pork and stir-fry about ½ minute, separating the pork shreds until the meat color changes. Remove and set aside.

4. Use the same oil remaining in the pan for the shrimp. When the oil is very hot again, put the shrimp into it. Separate the shrimp pieces individually and stir until pink. Remove to the bowl with pork.

5. Add the shredded cabbage to the oil left in the pan. (Add more oil if needed). Stir and fry for a minute. Add ingredients (c). Cover with lid and cook about 2 minutes. Then return the pork and shrimp. Stir and add the bean sprouts, scallions and cook another ½ minute. If not salty enough, salt to taste. Drain this filling in a colander about 2 hours. When the filling is almost dry, add ingredients (d). Mix very well.

6. Divide the cooked filling into 20 portions. Place each portion on a sheet of the egg roll skin (about 1 inch from the edge facing you). Fold up slantwise like a Chinese package, only do not tuck in the last corner. See instructions and illustrations for rolling egg rolls.

7. Heat the oil in a deep-frying pan over medium high heat or in an electric deep fryer at 350°F-375°F. (Drop a little piece of bread into the oil; if there are bubbles on the bread, the oil temperature is right.) The size of the fryer determines how many spring rolls can be fried simultaneously. Always turn the rolls, so all the sides are immersed in the oil (the upper side tends to float on the top of the oil). If the oil is too hot, turn the heat to medium. Fry until the skins are golden brown and crispy. Remove and drain on paper towels. Serve hot.

NOTE: 1. The spring rolls can be frozen and fried again about 5 minutes before serving.
2. The spring rolls can be kept warm in the oven before serving.

DOILIES (CHINESE PANCAKES)

3 cups sifted flour
1¼ cups boiling water
2 tbsp. vegetable, corn, or
** sesame oil**

1. Mix the flour and boiling water with a wooden spoon or chopsticks. When it is cool enough to touch, knead the dough smoothly about 5-10 minutes. If it is too dry, add 1-2 tablespoons of boiling water. Cover with a damp cloth and let stand at least one hour.

2. On a lightly floured surface, roll the dough into a long round stick about 12 inches long. Divide it into 24 portions. Make each into a flat cake about 2-inches in diameter. Brush one side of the cake with oil. Lay another cake on top of it. Roll the two together with a rolling pin, rotating the pancake an inch or so in a clockwise direction, so as to roll and form a double circular pancake of about 6-7 inches in diameter. Repeat the same with the other pieces. Cover with a lightly dampened cloth to keep from drying.

3. Heat a flat pan or griddle over medium heat about 1-2 minutes. When the pan gets hot, put the cake on it. When the cake puffs up and a little bubble appears on the surface or when light brown spots form on one side (about 2 minutes), turn over for about ½-1 minute. The heat should be checked frequently so it does not get too high or too low. (If medium heat becomes too high, turn the heat lower.) Pull the cooked cakes carefully apart into two very thin cakes. Pile up and cover with a cloth to keep the edges from drying until ready to steam. Remove the cloth and put the cakes on a dish in a steamer over medium high heat for 8-10 minutes. Do not let them touch the water while steaming. Serve immediately.

NOTE: 1. If you do not use the pancakes immediately, wrap them in aluminum foil and put in a plastic bag to freeze until needed. When needed, thaw and either steam for 8-10 minutes or put in 350° F oven for 8-10 minutes.

2. These pancakes can be used for serving Peking Duck and Moo Shi Meat.

八寶飯

EIGHT TREASURE RICE PUDDING

1½ cups glutinous rice
½ cup sweet red bean paste

(a) 1 tbsp. lard
     2 tbsp. sugar

(b) 10 dates
  10-15 cooked lotus seeds
     20 raw peanuts
     20 candied cherries
     10 walnut halves
     60 brown raisins
     10 red, green, or natural
        pineapple chunks
     ¼ cup candied orange peels

1 tbsp. lard
1 cup water
3 tbsp. sugar

(c) 1 tbsp. water
     1 tbsp. cornstarch

1. Wash the rice and drain well. Place in a deep pot. Add 1½ cups of cold water. Bring to boil over medium high heat. After the water boils, turn to low and cover. Simmer about 12 minutes or until done. Remove to a bowl and add ingredients (a). Stir and mix well.

2. Use a 6-8-inch heatproof bowl. Brush the bottom with 1 tbsp. lard and lay all of ingredients (b) decoratively in rows or other designs.

3. Place ⅔ of the mixed rice in the bowl, carefully covering the fruits and nuts. Then put the sweet red bean paste in the center. Cover the bean paste with the remaining rice, flattening it. Place the bowl in a steamer (see chapter 1) and steam the pudding about 1 hour or until done. Invert on a serving platter.

4. Boil 1 cup water in pan, add 3 tbsp. sugar, and make it sticky with a paste of ingredients (c). After the mixture thickens, pour over the pudding. Serve immediately.

NOTE: 1. You can make the red bean paste yourself. Wash and soak ½ cup dried red beans overnight. Drain and place in saucepan with water over medium high heat. When it boils, turn to low heat and simmer until very soft (about 1½-2 hours). Put the beans and the cooking liquid through a sieve. Pour the mixture into a deep saucepan and cook over medium high heat about ½ hour, stirring frequently. Add 3 tbsp. lard and about ¼ cup sugar or more (to your taste) into the mixture and continue cooking, stirring almost constantly for 10-15 minutes until the mixture becomes thick and looks like bean soup.

2. You can use assorted dried and candied fruits, such as cherries, angelica, figs, dates (for decoration) in addition to or in place of ingredients (b).

12

MISCELLANY

辣椒汁

HOT SAUCE

1 cup vegetable oil or corn oil
3 or 4 tbsp. crushed dry red hot
  pepper
4 tbsp. dry shrimp

(a)   ¾ cup chopped preserved
       turnip
    ¾-1 cup fermented black beans
     2 tbsp. sugar
     ½ tbsp. paprika
     ¼ tsp. garlic powder
     ½ tsp. salt
     ¼ tsp. ginger powder

(b)   ½ cup chopped scallions
     ½ tsp. monosodium gluta-
     mate (optional)

1. Soak the dry shrimp in hot water for 10 minutes, drain, and add to ingredients (a).

2. Heat the oil in a frying pan over medium high heat. When the oil is hot, put the crushed dry red hot pepper into it. Stir it about ½ minute. Add ingredients (a) and stir for a minute. Add ingredients (b), stir, remove from heat and let cool.

3. Put and store in a glass jar for use.

NOTE: This sauce is delicious with hot dogs, hamburger, pizza, spaghetti, rice, noodles, meatballs, meat loaf and other hot or cold meats (including sea food).

葡萄汁
PLUM SAUCE

1 lb. plums
1 cup water
2 tbsp. sugar
4 tbsp. soy sauce

1. Wash plums and remove the stones.

2. Place the plum meat with 1 cup of water in a pot over medium high heat. Bring to boil. Turn the heat to low. Simmer plums for ¾ to 1 hour. Strain the plum sauce through sieve into a clean pot, add the sugar and the soy sauce, and stir. Heat gently at low heat for another ¼ hour, stirring constantly until done.

3. Put into a glass jar and store in the refrigerator.

NOTE: This sauce is delicious with egg rolls and roast duck.

油炒冬菇
STIR-FRY MUSHROOMS

 2 lbs. fresh mushrooms
 2 cups vegetable oil
14 slices fresh ginger root
 2 tbsp. soy sauce
 ¾ tsp. salt or salt to taste

1. Wash and clean the mushrooms individually and thoroughly. Drain and cut into slices along the stems to the caps (T shaped).

2. Put paper towels on big cookie sheet. Spread the mushroom slices on it. Let dry 1-1½ days. Turn the slices several times.

3. Heat 2 cups oil in a frying pan over medium high heat. When the oil is hot, add the mushroom slices. Stir-fry a few seconds and add the ginger, soy sauce and salt. Stir-fry until all the water has evaporated.

4. Store in a jar for use. Stir-fry mushrooms can be substituted in recipes requiring dried Chinese mushrooms or used as seasonings for recipes needing mushrooms. Stir-fry mushrooms can be stored in the refrigerator for a couple of months.

13

SHOPPING GUIDE

You will find the shopping easier if you use the English spelling of the Chinese names for the ingredients. (The Chinese names are printed next to the English translation.) Many of the ingredients may require a special trip to a Chinese grocery store or a mail order. Since many of these ingredients are bought in cans and can be stored for quite awhile, the most efficient method of shopping entails stocking up on the ingredients in one huge mail order or shopping trip. When doing Chinese cooking, if an ingredient or a reasonable substitute is not available, the best thing to do is to omit it from the recipe.

1. Aduki Beans (Red Beans)   Hung Dow   紅豆

These red colored beans are sold in paper bags in a health food store or Chinese grocery.

2. Agar Agar, Dried   Yang Choy   洋菜

Agar Agar is bought in dried white strips in a bundle about 13 inches long. By separating some of the fibers and holding them under cold running water, the agar agar becomes loosened, translucent, and slippery strips. Cut them into 2 or 3-inch sections and cold-mix with shredded vegetables or ham strips to make cold salad dishes. Agar Agar is sold by the ounce in dried bundles wrapped with paper in a Chinese grocery and can be stored indefinitely at room temperature.

3. Bamboo Shoots   Tung Suehn   冬笋

Bamboo shoots are bought in cans or fresh whole or cut shoots which are found in water containers in a Chinese grocery. If canned bamboo shoots are used, after opening drain and store the shoots in fresh water in a covered jar in the refrigerator. By changing the water every few days, the bamboo shoots can be kept for about 2 weeks. Canned bamboo shoots can also be bought in many supermarkets.

4. Barley   Yü Mie   玉米

Barley is sold in paper bags in any supermarket.

5. Bean Curd, Fresh   Dow-foo   豆腐

Fresh bean curd is white with the texture of well-baked custard. It is sold individually by the square block in a Chinese grocery. The bean curd comes in water and should be drained and stored in fresh water in a covered jar in the refrigerator. The bean curd can be kept for up to two weeks by changing the water every 2 or 3 days.

6. Bean Curd, Dried   Fou Chu   腐竹

Dried bean curd is found in two shapes, either long folding strips or 3½ by 5-inch rectangular pieces. The bean curd is sold in paper packages in a Chinese grocery and can be stored at room temperature for months.

7. Bean Curd, Soft Dried   五香豆腐干
           Wu Hsiang Dow Foo Gan

This is bean curd which has been marinated in a mixture of soy sauce and five spices and become brown colored squares. It is sold individually in a Chinese grocery and can be kept in the refrigerator about a week.

8. Bean Curd, Fried   Yu Dow Foo Go   油豆腐果

Fried bean curd comes in small cubes and its color is light or golden brown. It can be sold individually or by the dozen in a Chinese grocery and can be frozen or stored in a refrigerator for a week.

9. Bean Sprouts   Dow Ya   豆芽

Bean Sprouts can be bought fresh or canned in a Chinese grocery or in most supermarkets. Fresh bean sprouts can be kept in a refrigerator for a couple of days.

10. Bird's Nest   Yen Wo   燕窩

Bird's nests are coated by Asian swiftlets and are fragments of a translucent gelatinous material. It is sold in ounces in a Chinese grocery and needs no refrigeration.

11. Black Fermented Beans, Dried   Dow Shih   豆豉

Black fermented beans are strongly flavored black soybeans which are sold in cans or plastic bags in a Chinese grocery. After opening, store in a tightly-covered container.

12. Chinese Cabbage   Bok Choy   白菜

Chinese Cabbage is also called chard cabbage because it looks like Swiss cabbage and consists of a clump of snow-white stalks ending in wide, dark green leaves. It is sold in a Chinese grocery or an oriental market and can be stored in the refrigerator for about a week.

13. Brown Bean Sauce   Yen Sei Shih   原晒豉

Brown bean sauce is a thick sauce made from fermented yellow beans, flour and salt. It is sold in 1-lb. cans in a Chinese grocery. After opening, the sauce can be stored in a covered jar in the refrigerator for months.

14. Bean Threads   Fun See   粉絲

Bean threads are thin, translucent noodles made from ground mung beans and are also called cellophane noodles or vermicelli. They are dried in looped skeins and sold in 2-6-ounce bundles in a Chinese grocery. Wrap well to store indefinitely at room temperature.

15. Brown Gravy Syrup   Tsu Yue   珠油

Brown gravy syrup is a brown colored sauce which is sold in jars in a Chinese grocery or supermarket. After opening, it can be stored in the refrigerator for weeks.

16. Celery Cabbage   Tienking Bok Choy   天津白菜

Celery cabbage is also called Chinese cabbage and consists of a solid, oblong head of wide, celerylike stalks ending in frilly, pale green leaves. It is sold in a Chinese grocery or most supermarkets and can be stored in the refrigerator for about a week.

17. Chinese Parsley   Yuan Sai   芫茜

Chinese parsley is an aromatic herb with flat leaves and a stronger flavor than the curly parsley. It is really the coriander spice plant which you can grow by planting whole coriander seeds. It can be bought in a Chinese grocery.

18. Chinese Noodles   Mein   麵

Chinese noodles are long thin noodles no more than ⅛ inch wide, made of flour, eggs and water. The noodles are sold by the pound, fresh or

163

dried in a Chinese grocery or noodles shop. Fresh noodles may be stored in plastic bags in the freezer for months or in the refrigerator for 1 week.

19. Chinese Dried Mushrooms   Doong Gwoo   冬菇

Chinese dried mushrooms are strongly-flavored dried mushrooms about 1-2 inches in diameter. They are sold in plastic bags, paper boxes or by weight in a Chinese grocery. If stored in a covered jar or tightly-sealed plastic bag, the mushrooms can be stored indefinitely at room temperature.

20. Duck Sauce   Soh Mai Jeong   蘇梅醬

Duck sauce is also called plum sauce and is a spicy accompaniment to roast duck or egg rolls. It is sold in 1-lb. cans or 4-12-ounce bottles in a Chinese grocery or gourmet shop. After opening, the sauce can be kept in a covered jar in the refrigerator for months.

21. Egg Roll Skin   Chun Chuan Pi   春捲皮

Egg roll skin consists of flour and egg and is made into 7-inch squares (the thinner, the better). It is sold by the pound in a Chinese grocery. By wrapping and storing in plastic bags, the skins can be stored in the freezer for months or in the refrigerator for a few days.

22. Five-spice Powder   Wu Hsiang Fun   五香粉

Five-spice powder is a blend of ground cloves, fennel, licorice, cinnamon and star anise, giving a strong aroma. It is sold in jars or bottles in a Chinese grocery and is stored at room temperature in tightly covered containers.

23. Ginger Root   Geung   薑

Ginger root adds flavor to all the dishes. A large amount of fresh ginger root, raw or cooked, is very hot and nippy, but a little merely enhances the flavor. The ginger root is sold by weight in a Chinese grocery or supermarket. It is stored in the refrigerator unwrapped for several months or in jars with sherry for many months.

24. Gingko Nuts   Boak Gwooh   白菓

Gingko nuts resemble garbanzo beans in color and flavor and are sold dried in plastic bags or jars, or shelled in cans in a Chinese grocery. After opening canned gingko nuts, store in a covered jar in the refrigerator.

25. Glutinous Rice   Noh Mai   糯米

Glutinous rice, when cooked, becomes a special sticky rice. It is sold in 5-lb. bags or by weight in a Chinese grocery. Store in a covered container at room temperature.

26. Hoisin Sauce   Hoi Sin Jeong   海鮮醬

Hoisin sauce is a sweet, brownish-red sauce used as a seasoning or accompaniment to Peking Duck. It is sold in 1-lb. cans or jars in a Chinese grocery. After opening, the sauce can be stored in a tightly-covered container in the refrigerator for months.

27. Hot Bean Sauce (Hot Soy Bean Paste)   四川豆瓣醬
       Szechuan La Dow   Ban Jeong

Hot bean sauce, also called Szechuan hot sauce, is a sauce or paste made of soy beans and hot pepper. It is sold in a Chinese grocery.

28. Jellyfish   Shui Mu   水母

Jellyfish has a body of jellylike consistency and is salted and stored in plastic bags. Before using, soak in water for several hours or overnight. Wash away the salt and cut into shreds to cold-mix with vegetables as a salad. It is sold by the pound in a Chinese grocery and can be kept in the refrigerator for several months.

29. Kumquats   Gen Jou   金橘

Kumquats are a Chinese citrus fruit which is yellow-orange in color and has a tart orange flavor. They are sold in cans or jars in a Chinese grocery. After opening, store in their original syrup in a tightly-covered jar in the refrigerator.

30. Lichee Nuts   Lie Chee   荔枝

Lichee nuts are oval, the outer covering hard and scaly, and the seed small and hard. The flesh surrounding the seed, when dried, is firm, sweetish and black, constituting the edible part of the so-called lichee nuts of commerce. They are sold fresh (in early summer) and dried in shells, or canned in syrup in a Chinese grocery. After opening canned lichee nuts, store in original syrup in a covered jar in the refrigerator.

31. Loquats   Pee Pun   枇杷

Loquats are a small plumlike fruit with a peachlike flavor and yellow-orange color. They are sold pitted and preserved in cans in a Chinese grocery. After opening, store in original syrup in a covered jar in the refrigerator.

32. Lotus Seeds   Lian Jee   蓮子

Lotus seeds are shaped like dried white corn kernels and sold in plastic packages or shelled in cans in a Chinese grocery. After opening, the canned lotus seeds should be stored in a covered jar in the refrigerator.

33. Monosodium Glutamate   Wei Gin   味精

Monosodium glutamate is also called Accent or gourmet powder and is used to enhance the flavor of the food. It is sold in cans, bottles or jars in a Chinese grocery or supermarket. It can be kept in a tightly-covered container for months at room temperature.

34. Mung Beans (Green Beans)   Lü Dow   綠豆

Mung beans are sold in paper bags in a health food store or Chinese grocery.

35. Mustard Greens   Gai Choy   芥菜

Mustard Greens consist of a clump of fat apple-green stalks ending in darker apple-green leaves. It has a mustard flavor and is sold in a Chinese grocery or in some farmers' markets. It can be stored in a plastic bag in the refrigerator for a few days.

36. Mustard Greens, Pickled   Suan Choy   酸菜

Pickled mustard greens are green cabbage-like vegetables packed in brine. The greens are sold in cans, jars or from barrels in a Chinese grocery and can be stored in a covered container in the refrigerator for several weeks.

37. Oyster Sauce   Hou Yu   蠔油

Oyster sauce is a thick brown sauce with a rich flavor made from oysters, soy sauce and brine. It is sold in 6- or 12-ounce bottles in a Chinese grocery and can be kept in tightly-closed bottles at room temperature indefinitely.

38. Pork Sausage   Lop Cheong   腊腸

Pork sausage is about 5 inches long and must be simmered or steamed 15 minutes or until the fat is translucent. It is sold by weight in a Chinese grocery and can be stored in plastic bags in the refrigerator for months.

39. Red Bean Paste   Hung Dow Sah   紅豆沙

Red bean paste is a thick sweet paste made from red beans. It is sold in cans in a Chinese grocery and can be stored after opening in a covered container in the refrigerator for months.

40. Red Dates   Hung Joh   紅棗

Red dates have a patent-leathery maroon color and are sold in plastic bags in a Chinese grocery. They are stored in a plastic or any covered container at room temperature for months.

41. Salted Eggs   Hahm Dahn   鹹蛋

Salted eggs are duck eggs which have been brine-cured. Cook 20-30 minutes before shelling. The eggs are sold individually in a Chinese grocery and can be stored in the refrigerator about 3-4 weeks.

42. Sesame Seeds   Chih Mah   芝蔴

Sesame seeds are tiny flat seeds either black or white. They are sold in plastic bags in a Chinese grocery and are stored in a covered container at room temperature.

43. Sesame Seed Oil   Mah Yue   芝蔴油

Sesame seed oil is a strong-flavored oil made from sesame seeds. It is sold in jars or in cans in a Chinese grocery and will keep indefinitely at room temperature if stored in a tightly-covered container.

44. Shark's Fin   Yee Tze   魚翅

Shark's fin is a long thread of dried cartilage from the fins of sharks. It is sold by weight in 6-8-ounce boxes or already cooked in a sauce in cans in a Chinese grocery. It will keep indefinitely.

45. Shrimp, Dried   Hsia Mie   蝦米

Dried shrimp are tiny shelled and dried shrimp with a sharp, salty flavor. They are sold in 4-8-ounce plastic bags in a Chinese grocery and can be stored in a covered jar at room temperature for months.

46. Smithfield Ham   Hoh Twen   火腿

Smithfield is not Chinese, but close in taste to Chinese ham. It is sold by weight or by slices in a Chinese grocery or gourmet shop and can be stored in the refrigerator for several weeks by wrapping tightly in foil or plastic bags.

47. Snow Peas   Sih Dow   雪豆

Snow peas are flat, pale-green peas which are cooked and eaten unshelled. They are sold fresh by weight in a Chinese grocery and some farmers' markets and frozen in 10-ounce boxes in supermarkets. Fresh snow peas are stored in plastic bags in the refrigerator for 1-2 weeks.

48. Soy Sauce   Jeong Yue   醬油

Soy sauce is a basic ingredient in Chinese cooking. Chinese soy sauce is the saltiest and made almost entirely from beans. The Japanese soy sauce is less salty and sweeter due to the addition of a large amount of toasted wheat. Several Chinese soy sauces are imported. Sang Chow is lighter in color than the Japanese and is good for stir-frying. Low Chow, which is darker with a slight molasses and bitter taste, is good for red-cooking food. These soy sauces are sold in cans and bottles in a Chinese grocery or supermarket and can be stored in a covered container at room temperature for months.

49. Star Anise   Balt Ghok   八角

Star anise is a licorice-flavored spice with a beautiful 8-pointed star (an inch across) shape. It is sold in plastic bags in a Chinese grocery and can be stored in tightly-covered containers indefinitely.

50. Szechuan Peppercorn   Hwa Chow   花椒

Szechuan Peppercorns are brown speckled peppercorns with a mildly hot flavor with a pleasant scent. They are sold whole by weight in a Chinese grocery and can be kept indefinitely in a tightly-covered container.

51. Szechuan Preserved Cabbage   Tzuh Choy   榨菜

Szechuan preserved cabbage has a hot and strongly-pickled flavor. It is sold in cans in a Chinese grocery. After opening, it can be stored in a covered jar in the refrigerator for months.

52. Tapioca   Shi Mie   西米

There are two kinds of tapioca: one is smaller than rice, the other kind consists of little white balls. Tapioca is sold in a Chinese grocery, health-food shop and supermarket and can be kept indefinitely in a covered container at room temperature.

53. Thousand-Year Old Eggs   Pay Dahn   皮蛋

Thousand-year old eggs are duck eggs which have been coated with a paste of ashes, lime and salt and roasted in the ground for several months. The eggs are sold individually in a Chinese grocery and can be kept about 2-3 months.

54. Vegetable Steak   Mein Gin   麵筋

Vegetable steak looks like small fried cubed bean curd, but is made from wheat glutin. It is sold in cans in a Chinese grocery, oriental market or health-food shop.

55. Tiger Lily Stems, Dried   Gin Tseug   黃花(金針)

Dried tiger lily stems are pale-gold lily stems about 2-3 inches long. They are sold by weight or in plastic bags in a Chinese grocery and can be stored in a covered container for months.

56. Water Chestnuts   Mah Tai   馬蹄

Water chestnuts have brown scaly skins and look something like narcissus bulbs. They have white crispy meat and are sold fresh by weight or in various-sized cans (whole, sliced, or diced) in a Chinese grocery or in most supermarkets. After opening, canned water chestnuts should be stored in fresh water in a covered jar and can be kept for about a month by changing the water every 2-3 days.

57. White Radishes   Baak Loh Puh   白蘿葡

White radishes are very crispy, tender, mild and sweet and much like a turnip in flavor. They are sold by weight in a Chinese grocery or supermarket and can be stored for several days, if refrigerated in plastic bags.

58. Winter Melon   Doong Gwah   冬瓜

Winter melon resembles a watermelon, but its flesh is white, translucent and firmer. It is sold fresh in slices by weight in a Chinese grocery and can be kept in the refrigerator for several days with the cut surface covered with plastic wrap.

59. Won Ton Skin   Won Ton Pie   雲吞皮

Won ton skin is approximately 3½ inches square and made from flour and egg. Egg roll skins divided into quarters can be substituted and used as won ton skins (the thinner, the better). These (and won ton skin) are sold by weight in pounds in a Chinese grocery and can be kept in the refrigerator for several days or kept frozen for months by wrapping tightly in plastic bags.

60. Wood Ears   Moo Rh
                      Yin Rh   木耳(雲耳)

Wood ears are small, crinkly, gelatinous dried fungus, about 1-inch long. They are sold by weight in plastic bags in a Chinese grocery and kept indefinitely in a covered jar.

14

INDEX

Recipe Notes

Recipe Notes